W9-CNQ-238

Sets
and
Borders

by
Gwen Marston & Joe Cunningham

American Quilter's Society

Credits

Graphics by Joe Cunningham and his Amiga computer.
Photographs by The KEVA Partnership, Flint, Michigan.

Dedicated

This book is dedicated to Mary and Fred.

Table of Contents

Introduction

In the world of quiltmaking, the word "set" has meanings Mr. Webster never imagined. Generally, "the set of a quilt" refers to the way its components — usually blocks — are put together. We said "usually" blocks, because some quilts are made of only one patch, like GRANDMOTHER'S FLOWER GARDEN or TRIP AROUND THE WORLD and they have a set made of a single patch, not a block. Hence, they are examples of "One-Patch" sets. Then again, some quilts are made mostly of borders, not blocks. Their set is called "Medallion". Ordinarily, quilts are made of blocks and the blocks are "set" together, giving the finished quilt a "set". Some old-time quilters talked about setting blocks as in, "I'm getting ready to set my quilt," or, "Look at how those blocks are set!"

Often, the set of a quilt goes unnoticed and the blocks get all the glory. Only when a set is clever or wild enough to draw attention to itself do we single it out for comment. But sets require just as much thought and care as blocks or borders. While some sets offer few options, such as the One-Patch, many blocks can be set in an infinite variety of ways. It can be very convenient to learn how to do one set well and use it for all your quilts. Convenience, however, can be the enemy of creativity. Learning and using new sets can be just as fascinating, just as rewarding, as learning to make new blocks. Of course, the more sets you know, the more options you have when it comes time to make your next quilt.

Sampler quilts, for example, according to current fashion, are made with the same-size blocks, set together on the straight with plain sashing and given a plain border. A brief look at old sampler quilts shows that these standards are new. Old samplers were as often set on the diagonal as on the straight, often with no sashing and often with rich pieced or appliqued borders. Or consider two common contemporary sets, block-to-block and lattice-striped. One way to make your quilt stand out from the crowd is to use another set . . . **any** other set. The Streak of Lightning set is

almost extinct. Few applique borders survive. These ideas are out of fashion today — all the more reason to use them.

Sets can be everything blocks are: wild or tame, complex or simple, plain or fancy. Sets have the power to transform blocks into something wholly different than what they are by themselves. When we first became interested in sets we were astonished at those we found in antique quilts and tops. Today, however, we see fewer sets, of less variety. This is partly because the very notion of "a set" is disappearing from some areas of quiltmaking.

As quilts become increasingly identified with "art," they increasingly begin to resemble art in their composition. Thus, we see more and more quilts that are composed like paintings — as personal images put together in a pictorial format. Quilts made like this need no set as such. Only when "old-fashioned" quilts are the goal do we see the kinds of sets that are currently out of fashion: the Four-Block, the Random Sampler, Pieced Lattice and others. Some have survived and even flourished: Medallion, One-Patch and Plain Lattice, for instance.

For the most part, though, looking at old quilts makes us aware of how differently quilts are made today. And it brings up questions about those differences. Why are so many old quilts set in a way that looks out of balance? Why do so many have two or three-sided borders? Or half blocks along one side? Or misplaced groups of dark scraps? We think the answers to these and other questions about old quilts are in the way we view quilts, in both senses of the word.

From our studies of old quilts and discussions with older quilters, we have come to feel that seeing quilts on a bed and seeing them flat out on a wall are two entirely different experiences.

The difference is in how quilts are visualized. Because most of us have seen thousands of quilts in books, we have learned to visualize them primarily as flat and fully spread out. When we visualize a quilt we have seen or a quilt we might make, we see it as if we were the photographer, taking a picture of it hanging on a wall. This is consistent with the view that quilts are art and should be treated as such. Art hangs on the wall. Similarly, the accepted way to show quilts in books is as if the quilts were pictures: flat out and without a background, as they are in this book.

It is obvious that many antique quilts were visualized by their makers in the same way. Careful and artful symmetries, perfectly engineered resolutions at all corners — these attributes are not built into quilts by accident. And it is just as obvious that many quilts **were not** visualized flat out, but placed on a bed, perhaps on a particular bed.

If the quiltmaker is making a quilt to go on a bed, many of the "rules" of two-dimensional symmetry do not apply. A quilt's design has different meanings on a bed than on a wall. When it is on a bed, only part of a quilt can be seen at any one time; on the wall it can be seen corner to corner. On the bed a quilt is an attempt to beautify a home; on the wall it is a statement — a "work." On the bed it is three dimensional — on the wall, two. Perhaps we should go further and say that on the bed it has even more than three dimensions, because many quilts were made for very personal reasons, made to please and have meaning for the quiltmaker's family. Once again, the absence of background is the most significant difference between the two ways of viewing a quilt.

In order to survive in the highly competitive contemporary art arena, quilts must be able to stand on their own in a gallery, without background, accompanied only by technical information. Contemporary art quilts made by quilt artists are made to be displayed this way, labeled only by title, artist, date, materials and dimensions. And, as we have said, most old quilts stand on their own like this very well indeed, even though some have many artistically inexplicable elements. These elements come because the quiltmaker was thinking about things other than the design. For instance: it may have been more important for the fabric from a certain blue dress to be included in a quilt than how it would look in the quilt. Because someone in a hurry ran out of red for the border, she substituted various, handy browns. She might have wanted to reproduce a pattern she saw at the fair last year but did not know how to draft, ending up with a skewed original design. Or she might have decided that the quilt she was making for the upstairs bedroom should only have fancy borders on one side and the top, because the bed could not be pulled away from the wall and "you can't get the quilt down between there and it would be a devil to make, so the only way it will lay right is if I . . ." These are the decisions that lead to quilts. They are not necessarily the decisions that lead to art.

What does this have to do with sets? Everything. When you think about the blocks for your next quilt,

you will already have an image in your mind — however tentative and shadowy — of how the quilt will look when it is finished. The chances are that you will picture it in one of two settings: on the wall or on the bed. In some ways at least, the way you picture it indicates for whom you are making it, your audience. If you picture it on the wall, most decisions you make as you construct your quilt will be based on the answer to one main question: "How will it **look**?" If you picture your next quilt on someone's bed, however, your decisions might rather be based on your feelings for that person in particular and you might include elements in it that will only be fully understood by them. We want to encourage you to visualize your quilt in any setting you want — at home or in the gallery.

About This Book

This book is not intended to be a complete encyclopedia of designs. Rather, we hope it will stimulate you to keep your own file of ideas and to try one of these on your next quilt. Also, we want to make clear that the technical instructions are a result of our experiences making many quilts, not the result of our study of contemporary technique. So it is likely that some of our instructions will differ from those you will see elsewhere. That is how it should be: we all must find our own ways of working. A large part of the uniqueness and vitality seen in antique quilts was a result of individual quilters working out their own responses to design problems instead of following an official set of rules. This book is a review of the tradition — our tribute to the long line of American quiltmakers.

We encourage you to be creative by making quilts in your own way, to trust your own instincts, to find out what kind of quilt you enjoy making and make it. That is what this book is really about: finding your own way of working. We hope you will find these set and border ideas as much fun to explore as we have.

About These Quilts

The quilts in this book are from our collection and from the Mary Schafer Collection. Some are antique quilts and some were made by us or by Mary. They are arranged in alphabetical order for easy reference, so you must check the captions to find out who made each one.

Our quilts represent our ongoing study of old quilts for little-used ideas that we can appropriate. Therefore, nearly anything you might see in one of our quilts that looks new or original probably comes from an idea we ran across on an antique quilt. After making well over one-hundred quilts, all different, we find ourselves in the same position in which we started: with many more ideas than we will ever have time to use.

We piece our quilts on the machine and do all our applique and quilting by hand. We use only 100% cotton fabric and thread. Our batting is usually the Fairfield Cotton Classic, which we sometimes split into one-half thickness. Some of these quilts have cotton flannel for batting and some have 100% cotton batting. The rest have various polyester batts, usually Poly-Fil.

Mary Schafer has been making quilts since 1948. We have known her since the mid-70s, and as her close friends and custodians of her collection, we have benefitted from her advice and broad knowledge of the tradition. Her quilts were perfect for this book, as most of them have beautiful border designs. In fact, much of what makes Mary's quilts so extraordinary is in her original borders — perfectly engineered complements to the blocks and beautiful frames for the quilts. Original though they are, those borders also reflect Mary's steadfast devotion to the traditional style as she sees it. She, too, continues to find new ideas faster than she can use them, even though she works at a feverish pace.

Some of the quilts are listed as being by "Elizabeth Harriman and Mary Schafer." Betty Harriman was a great quiltmaker and collector from Bunceton, Missouri. She and Mary were friends — through quilting — and when Betty died in 1971, Mary acquired all her unfinished work. Since that time she has completed twenty-four of the starts. Nineteen were actually begun by Betty; five were antique blocks or tops she had collected. For the whole story, see *Uncoverings, 1986*, published by the American Quilt Study Group, 105 Molino Ave., Mill Valley, CA.

Mary's quilts are completely hand-sewn. She uses cotton fabric and thread. Most of her quilts have polyester batting; some have cotton.

About These Patterns

Most of the patterns in this book are taken from old quilts. Our cut-off date was 1940 and the great majority of quilts we studied were from 1825-1900. We drew on our own collection of antique quilts and our records of border and set ideas taken from old quilts. As custodians of the Schafer Collection, we have become familiar with her large holding of fine antique quilts. The books listed in our bibliography represent our favorite references. Because it is sometimes difficult to visualize what a pattern will look like when made up, we offer a reference section so that you can find a quilt with the pattern you are interested in.

During the course of our studies, some designs we had thought were our own original ideas turned up in old quilts--a reminder that almost everything has been tried.

Beginnings

It has sometimes been suggested that patchwork quilts and the Blues (or Jazz) are the only art forms to have originated in North America. That is an appealing idea, especially to quilters and blues or jazz musicians. Unfortunately, it is not precisely accurate. Blues music certainly had its origin here, and quiltmaking flourished. But quilts, even quilts made of many small pieces sewn together, were made in Europe and China long before being made here. What **was** begun here was a new block-style of quiltmaking. Prior to the invention of the quilt block—the small, repeated unit that forms the quilt top—quilts were usually made of whole cloth, so the entire quilt consisted of one design, not a series of repeated blocks.

Once the block was composed, sets had to be devised. (It is much more difficult to say, "Blues and the block style of quiltmaking, together with certain sets and quilting ideas . . ." than it is to say, "Patchwork quilts and the Blues . . .") And they were devised by the score. Like blocks, sets developed in a fairly logical progression from simple to complex. Generally, the oldest sets are the simplest.

The earliest quilts in this country were probably made of either plain or printed whole cloth. Few fabrics were wide enough for an entire top, so the majority of the early quilts were probably pieced somehow, perhaps with simple strips. From this practical solution to the problem of how to make bedcovers, three kinds of quilt designs could have developed.

First, was the whole-cloth design we know from early all-white quilts and linsey-woolseys. These could be made from homespun fabric. The design of these is carried out entirely with quilting stitches. Imported fabric, usually printed, was used as well, although early examples we have seen were less elaborately quilted than plain fabric quilts.

Second, were the simple Bars quilts made by seaming together two different prints or colors. Here we would have a practical decision leading to an artistic one. Practical, because quilts had to be made whether or not one had enough of one kind of fabric; artistic, because once a quilter had made the leap from one to more than one fabric, she would soon develop ideas about the kinds of fabrics that went together best, and even split one of the strips to make narrower strips for the sides.

Third, were the simple medallion designs made by adding a bottom or top strip to a Bars design. With these added strips, a "frame" could be created around the center of the quilt. We do not know the exact origin of this type of quilt, nor whether such utilitarian concerns had anything to do with its popularity. We think it is most likely the medallion happened to be easy to construct, as well as an imitation of the bedcovers arriving here from the East — part of the flourishing India trade.

During the seventeenth and eighteenth centuries a popular kind of bed covering was the "palampore," imported from India. Most palampores that have survived are finely woven cotton which was painted and embroidered with a "Tree of Life" design—an exotic, fantastical tree, decorated with animals, people, birds, etc., and framed with beautifully painted borders. Palampores were not usually quilted, but they almost certainly had a strong influence on quilt design. Fabric printers imitated Indian designs from palampores— flowers, leaves, plants, etc.—and quilters began to make quilts that imitated the palampore's "medallion" design. Apparently, these new quilts became popular around 1750 and remained so until 1810-1825.

The Medallion, or "framed-center" style that resembled a palampore, became the earliest "fad" in American quiltmaking. This style had several advantages in the New World where chintz was prohibitively expensive for many quilters. A fairly small piece of fancy chintz could be used for the center panel, while the surrounding borders could be made of more common cottons. Plain borders could be decorated with birds or flowers cut out of a small piece of expensive fabric, stretching it to cover much more area than if it were left whole. And when larger pieces of chintz could be found, they could be used whole or nearly whole in borders. Further, as the lush look of the palampore relied on dense pattern and design, pieced borders and applique borders were developed to imitate it. The vines which became so popular as applique border patterns may have begun as approximations of the fantastical vines on palampores.

Other fads would come and go as quilts changed with the times: Linsey-Woolsey quilts, Friendship quilts, Crazy quilts, Grandmother's Flower Garden and many others. Looking at quilt history as we worked on this book, we realized that the first big fad quilt, the Medallion, was also the first superstar quilt of the current revival.

At some point, no one really knows where, the quilt **block** became the primary unit from which quilts were designed and made. Some have suggested that all quilts made before 1750 were whole-cloth, that blocks only came into wide use around the Revolutionary War period. That may be. And it may be that the first few experiments with sets became the basis of the standard repertoire: block to block, alternate blocks, lattice, straight and diagonal.

Jonathan Holstein, in *The Pieced Quilt*, argues convincingly that the block style of quiltmaking was a functional solution to a design problem. He points out that pieced quilts were almost always made as "utility" quilts—unlike the fancy applique quilts for "best" use—which implies that all the steps in the construction process would be modified to make them as efficient as possible.

Small blocks, for instance, were efficient by using small scraps of fabric that would otherwise go to waste. Blocks of any size were efficient because they could be picked up whenever there was time. Whether or not sets played a role in making the process efficient, they were at least necessary if quilts were made of blocks. So sets evolved with blocks.

While few quilts from before 1800 have survived, the ones extant clearly show that the major set and border designs had all been developed by then. Of course, the innumerable block designs had yet to be composed and new kinds of sets and borders have been developed ever since. But with the block designs that were available, quilters were setting them together on the straight, on the diagonal, block to block, with alternate plain blocks, with lattice strips, in bars and medallions. Pieced borders were common, including the sawtooth variations which are still so popular. Applique borders were widely used, too, as well as combinations of the two techniques.

Applique quilts used the same general sets as pieced quilts. One set, however, was used almost exclusively for applique quilts—the Four Block. (We have seen several pieced examples, including a Four-Block linsey-woolsey, but most are appliqued.) According to a letter from Elizabeth Harriman to Mary Schafer in 1970, Four Block quilts may date from very early times, when much fabric was homespun:

"The 'Princess Feather' quilts were most always 4 block quilts and were square. I have read that the early appliqued quilts were always 4 blocks, 1 yd. square and were designed that way as it was easier to handle and the homepsun material was not cut up into small blocks."

We have never read this anywhere else. But there is something about the set that spawns unusual explanations. In *Old Patchwork Quilts*, Ruth Finley has this to say about it.

"These four-block quilts, which went out of patchwork style before 1850, would be the joy of the modern decorator, but though many were made in their day they are now difficult to find. They saw harder usage than those of small designs, because, taking less time to make, they could be replaced more easily. Also the vogue for them did not last long, their patterns being too bold to suit the genteel fancies of the middle nineteenth century."

Both women might be right. But we have never seen a Four-Block documented **before** 1850. And, while some large patterns may have been quicker to make than those of small designs, many of the Four-Blocks we have seen were framed with elaborate applique borders that would have taken as long as any. Our opinion is that Four-Blocks were made for a long time before 1850, and for a decade or two after. We have seen many PRINCESS FEATHER or PRINCESS PLUME quilts, (or WASHINGTON PLUME or PRINCE'S FEATHER) that were claimed to be from around 1800, and looked it. It seems that few were made after 1875 or so. Apparently their patterns are still too bold to suit the "genteel fancies of the day."

Another unusual set is the "Random" set. We think its origin could be something like this: A woman who quilted all her life would often make samples of different blocks, either projects started but not finished, or simply as the best way to "take notes" on a block. Because the majority of block patterns were developed during the nineteenth century, it would be near the end of that century that collections of varied blocks would become most common. When the quilter died, or when she wanted to distribute her earthly goods before she died, someone else would come into possession of the sample blocks. In an attempt to keep them all together, the new owner would just sew them all into a quilt top, regardless of pattern, color, size or shape of each block.

This would explain not only why so many of these quilts seem to have been made by two different quiltmakers, but also why they seem to appear only near the end of the nineteenth century.

Now, this might not be the way these Random set sampler quilts developed, but the ones we have seen do seem to fit the description: often made by two different people, usually dating from 1875-1900. Being such an unpredictable and unruly method of quiltmaking, it is not taught or discussed much in contemporary classes. But when we wanted to make one of these lively quilts, we merely followed the same sort of process that a quilter might have followed a hundred years ago.

So, with all the main concepts of how to get blocks together and how to make borders, it fell to the innumerable quilters to vary the details. Studying the quilts in our collection, in Mary Schafer's Collection and in all our quilt books, we have found nearly as many variations as quilts. But we have also found some general trends in sets and borders.

We have found that antique block-style quilts were most often set on the "straight." The most popular straight set was Block-to-Block. About one quarter of the quilts we looked at were set with some kind of lattice — the majority of which were set on the straight. Fewer were set with alternate plain blocks, and fewer still were Four-Block quilts. The least used set seems to have been the Bars set and its variations.

It is likely that the Block-to-Block, on the straight, was the most often used set merely because it was the most straightforward and logical way to use a bunch of square quilt blocks. If that is true, then it would seem that the least obvious way to use them would be the least used, and in our study, it was. Streak of Lightning, which requires that every other bar of blocks begin with a half block — and that uses triangles to create a zig-zag — was the rarest set in our group of quilts. One-half of one percent of the quilts we looked at were set this way. Easier sets show up more often than harder ones, exactly as you might expect.

The same is true of borders. About one-quarter of the antique quilts we have seen have no border, which is the easiest border of all. Next easiest is the plain band, or whole-cloth border, and about one-quarter of all quilts have them. So about one-half of the quilts we studied had plain borders or no borders at all. One reason for this was the important place reserved for quilted areas in nineteenth century quilts. Wide plain borders offer perfect opportunities for large-scale quilting designs. More than half the applique quilts had applique borders, and about one third of the pieced quilts had pieced borders. In about ten percent of the quilts, the opposite was true.

In general, borders developed from simple to complex just as sets did. Once the applique border became popular sometime around 1800, it became a common fixture of quiltmaking, with each quilter devising her own. Pieced borders were less flexible than applique, and they were much less varied. More than half of all pieced borders belong to the sawtooth family, and very few ever attained the complexity of fine applique borders.

A fairly wide outer border with a narrow inner border has become almost standard today, and most often these are made of whole cloth, not pieced or appliqued. When we looked at antique quilts to see when this format became popular, we were surprised to find very few examples before 1900. This kind of border is used on Amish quilts as well as some Pennsylvania German quilts from the nineteenth century. But only during the 1920s and '30s have we found this kind of format in general use.

Amish quilts, crazy quilts and crib quilts have their own qualities, much different than other kinds of quilts. For that reason we did not include these quilts in our studies. Other types of quilts also form sub-classes that make it difficult to generalize about sets and borders. Log Cabins, for example, are set together block to block almost 100% of the time. And nearly half had no border at all. Among the Log Cabins, though, we were able to see that BARN RAISING was the most popular set, accounting for one fourth of all quilts of the type. COURTHOUSE STEPS was next most common, followed by STRAIGHT FURROW, SUN AND SHADOW—all three sets were used more than ten percent of the time. ZIG-ZAG was the least often used. When Log Cabin quilts did have borders, the plain border was by far the most likely choice.

Sets

The "set" is the way the pieced or appliqued blocks are assembled to make up the quilt top. Like the fabric, pattern or quilting designs you choose, the set you decide to use for your quilt will be part of what determines its style. Certain sets look as old-fashioned as butter churns, which may be exactly what you want. Some can transform a quilt block from country cousin to downtown dandy. Let's take a look at some common and some not-so-common sets and see how they can make the same block seem plain or fancy, wild or tame, even straight or curved! For illustration of the designs we have decided to use a simple block pattern that has many names, including the one we use for it: "Savannah Star."

The simplest is the Block-to-Block, on the straight set, where the blocks are merely set side by side until they create a field wide enough and long enough. (a) Block-to-Block is a dense, busy-looking set that obscures the individual blocks. Where the blocks meet, new patterns appear. This is a popular set with contemporary quilters, because of the many design possibilities it allows. By using different shades of color, you can make a very contemporary-looking design with this simple block. By carefully arranging the darks and lights, you can create a three-dimensional effect easily. By scattering the shades all over, you can recreate the scrap quilt look of times past.

The first variation of this set happens when you turn the blocks one-quarter turn and set them Block-to-Block, "on the diagonal." (b) It hardly seems like the same block! The lines of the star points that seemed spiky and straight now look almost curved. You can vary the set with all the shadings from the first Block-to-Block set, and once again have a contemporary-looking piece, artful and elaborate, made with a simple block.

One effect of the Block-to-Block set that is not immediately apparent is that quilting is relegated to a supporting role in the quilt. With no open spaces to show off the quilting, it will be relatively unimportant to the finished piece. So one consideration when you choose your set should be whether or not you want the quilting to be an important part of the finished quilt.

If you **would** like the quilting to play a more prominent role in your quilt, you could "open up" the design by using the next variation on the Block-to-Block set: the "Alternate Plain Block" set. (c) With alternate plain blocks, each block maintains its own identity, the busy feeling of the block-to-block set disappears and the quilting designs become much more significant. The plain blocks will nearly disappear if they are the same color or print as the background of the pieced blocks. If they contrast with the pieced blocks, they will naturally be a more significant part of the design.

Alternate plain blocks are frequently used whether the set is on the straight or on the diagonal. If you plan to set your blocks on the diagonal the half and quarter blocks around the edge can be plain, much simpler than the Block-to-Block set where you must cut new templates for them.

Earlier in this century, it was fashionable to devise other alternate plain block variations like these. (d) We have seen many of these in our studies of old patterns, but few in actual quilts. This is one of our favorite devices, and even though it can look old-fashioned as in QUEEN CHARLOTTE'S CROWN, it can also be manipulated to seem very modern, as in BIRDS IN FLIGHT.

If you have made a block-style quilt, chances are you have used the next kind of set: lattice stripping, or "sashing." (e) "Stripping," as some older quilters we know call it, is one of the oldest of sets, and one that seems never to have gone out of fashion. One reason for that might be the almost endless variations possible with "stripping."

Lattice strips are often simply that: strips of colored or printed fabric. But they can just as easily be pieced or appliqued. They can be wide or narrow, with corner blocks or without, dark or light. Our next Savannah Star has lattice strips that work almost like alternate plain blocks, and seem to lay quietly in the background. (f)

This is yet another illustration of the infinite variety of quilt design, the reason why so few quilts are alike. Given a Savannah Star block pattern, no two of us would follow the same path through the maze of choices of color, pattern, set, border and quilting designs.

Plain sashing is most often used as a visual grid to "hold" the blocks in place, separate and individual. That is why most contemporary sampler quilts are set with sashing between the blocks; when all the blocks are different, it makes sense to insulate them from each other. Another, perhaps even more significant, reason is that it is hard to go wrong with plain lattice strips. Because of this, they are very common.

Less common is pieced lattice. While plain sashing usually stays in the background, pieced sashing can easily dominate the design. These kinds of strips are not used very often, perhaps because they seem more intimidating than plain strips, more difficult to handle. But, like many parts of quiltmaking, the only truly difficult part of using pieced sashing is deciding to. When you have decided to use pieced strips, it can be exciting to see a simple block become part of a dramatic design, merely by adding a lattice strip.

Of course, most pieced blocks would benefit little from the addition of a pieced lattice strip. But applique blocks with white space around them could often be enhanced with a bold pieced sashing. Speaking of bold pieced sashing, an uncommon and interesting use of pieced lattice is to use it for the whole quilt, with plain instead of patterned blocks. Since there is no other design to compete with, the lattice pattern can be as bold as you wish.

Appliqued lattice is fairly rare, perhaps because it seems like too much of a good thing. But it can be extremely effective, as it is in GRAPES AND VINES.

About as common as pieced lattice is the Bars set. (f) Once quite popular, Bars is little used today except in its well-known Amish manifestation. Some patterns were designed to be made only with a Bars set: TREE EVERLASTING, WILD GOOSE CHASE AND BARS, the Amish design, are the most popular—although there are others. Almost any block, however, could be set together this way.

A Bars set gives your quilt many of the same elements as an alternate plain block set: room for quilting, orderliness, a balance of positive and negative space. Among old quilts set this way, we have seen tremendous variation. With many possible sizes of plain blocks between the blocks in the bars, and the width, color or print of the plain bars, the variations are endless. Therefore, it is the least standardized of sets.

Even more rare is the Streak of Lightning set, which we classify as a Bars variation. (g) Unlike the regular Bars set, it has no plain strips—it has plain triangles instead. By starting every other column of blocks with a half block you make the triangles overlap to form zig-zags. If your fabric for the triangles is a light color the set will be unobtrusive. Darker or bolder prints or colors create a jagged, powerful set like no other.

a. The most often used method of sewing blocks together, whether by hand or by machine, is sewing them into rows, then joining the rows together to form the quilt top. This is our basic technique for all block-style quilts. As with most parts of quiltmaking, pins are your best friends in this. Pin all points you want to match. Pin along long seams to insure even sewing.

b. Diagonal sets are sewn in diagonal rows. Start with the partial block in the corner, then make the first row of a whole block and two triangles, or half-blocks as in this illustration. On many old quilts, the partial blocks were often made by cutting up a whole block, which accounts for nipped-off points and crooked edges. To make the half and quarter blocks fit correctly, you must cut new templates with seam allowances on all outside edges.

c. Alternate plain block sets are constructed the same as their Block-to-Block counterparts. In any set that uses triangular blocks, it is important that the outside edges be cut on the straight of fabric, so the long outside edges of the top will not stretch out of shape.

d. Unusual alternate plain block variation.

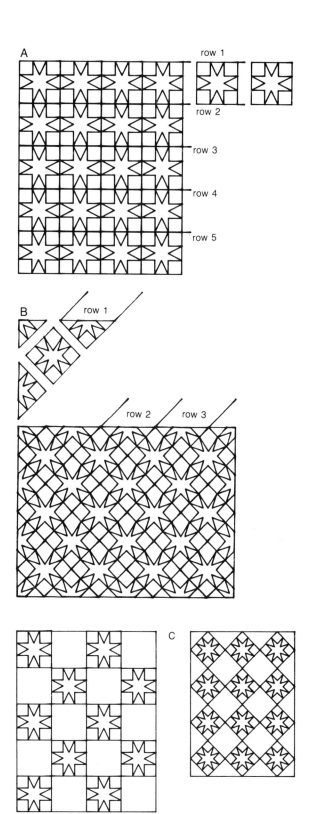

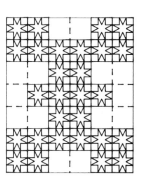

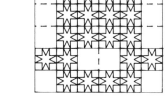

e. Even though you are careful in your construction of the blocks, you may find that their finished dimensions vary slightly. To keep this from becoming a problem, cut the lattice strips—or plain blocks—all the same size and make the pieced blocks fit. We have used all these methods for lattice stripping and think they'll work equally well. Use whichever one seems easiest or best for you.

f. The process is the same for a diagonal set. Once again, it is important to keep all outside edges of the top on the straight of the fabric.

g. The Bars set could be defined as alternate plain rows. These blocks are set on the diagonal, but they could be on the straight, with or without plain blocks between, with more borders or with none—this is one of the most flexible of all sets.

h. Streak of Lightning is a Bars variation—instead of alternate plain rows, the alternate rows begin with a half-block. Keep the grain of all plain triangles vertical.

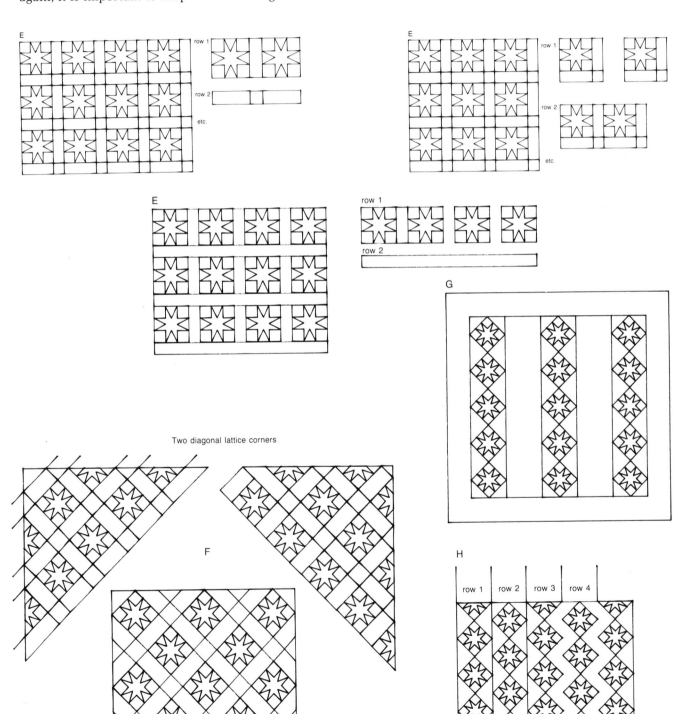

Two diagonal lattice corners

Borders

Nowhere is it written that you must have a border for your quilt. Our STREAK OF LIGHTNING NINE-PATCH has no border and needs none. Neither does our LOG CABIN. Perhaps your next quilt will also be pieced to the edges—but it is unlikely. The great majority of new quilts have borders of some kind, if only the narrowest strip. How do you decide what kind of border to use? Which border design goes well with your pattern? How can you design your own? In this section we will try to answer these questions and others, showing how you can emphasize, manipulate or downplay aspects of your overall design with your original borders.

The most common border is a simple band of whole cloth, like we used on the JACOB'S LADDER variation. It is used so often because pieced or appliqued borders would only interfere with many block patterns. A prime consideration in choosing what kind of whole cloth border to use should be the way you intend to quilt it. Wide plain borders invite elaborate quilting and they can look unfinished if the designs seem perfunctory. Wide **printed** borders will obscure your quilting designs. Plain and printed borders are indeed common today, but very wide or boldly printed borders are not. See how old-fashioned the Thousand Triangles border looks, for instance.

First cousin to the whole-cloth border is the border made of multiple bands. Here is another simple way to frame your quilt without extensive planning or work. Multiple bands are frequently used as "inner" and "outer" borders, with the outer being the widest. With this system the inner field of blocks is contained and complemented by the borders in much the same way as a picture is contained and complemented by a mat and frame. PRAIRIE QUEEN and MAY BASKET use this format.

Quilters have used any number of bands, wide and narrow. A border made of several strips can become an important part of the quilt's design, a sort of counterweight to a heavy interior.

"Interrupted borders" is our name for those that do not take 90 degree turns at the corners. Accustomed as we are to all borders being mitered, these interrupted borders can be jarring. Still, we find them refreshing reminders that the way we make quilts today is only one of the ways it can be done. There are many variations on this theme, but most have one thing in common: instead of each strip of a border being allowed to wend its way continuously around, two sides of the border will be finished before the other sides are begun. See the FOUR-PATCH CHAIN and CIRCULAR SAW for examples.

If you use a border other than simple bands of fabric, chances are you will use a pieced border. Pieced borders represent a vast category of both actual and potential patterns, as any pieced block contains elements that could be used for a pieced border design. These borders can be quite simple—squares sewn side by side—or extremely complex—mariner's blocks all around the edge.

The SAWTOOTH design and all it variations is probably the pieced border you see the most. The design we think of as "Basic Sawtooth" consists of right, isosceles triangles lined up on their short sides, alternating between light and dark. (A particular technical problem with this is the corner resolution, leading to the many chopped off triangles and strange shapes you find on older examples.) This border is almost infinitely adaptable—in size, formality, style and overall quilt design. Whether you are making an all original art quilt or a nineteenth-century Pennsylvania German style quilt, you could probably use a sawtooth border. Figures 1-20 show the Basic Sawtooth and some of its disguises.

The easiest variation of the Basic Sawtooth is the one we call the "Hypotenuse" version: simply flip the template over to its long side. (Fig. 20-21) By once again alternating the lights and darks, you create a pattern that looks much different than the Basic Sawtooth. It gives a more "open" effect than the Basic Sawtooth, as it used fewer triangles, fewer lines. Using two of these Hypotenuse strips together creates one of our favorite border patterns — Streak of Lightning. (Fig. 59-63) It is made exactly like the set of the same name and it can be just as electric.

WILD GOOSE CHASE is another pattern made of triangles, one large and one small. (Fig. 33-37) The WILD GOOSE CHASE you see most often is made of a rectangle twice as long as it is wide, but once again, any rectangle would work. If the rectangle is long and narrow, the "geese" can become odd-shaped and distorted, which might be just what you want.

A pattern that is even simpler is made of squares. (Fig. 49-58) It could be as straightforward as side-by-side squares. But the squares could be used grid-style to create many simple variations. Of course, many of these could be strip-pieced. Alphabets, pictures or abstract shapes can be easily pieced with squares.

Strip-piecing can work wonderfully well for borders; in fact strip-piecing was invented by the Seminole Indians to make border patterns of complex design easily. A design that may have been strip-pieced by traditional quilters was the strip border used for JOSEPH'S COAT quilt. (Fig. 64-65) We have used it on simple NINE-PATCH and LOG CABIN quilts, where it always looks at home. The strips may extend perpendicular to the body of the quilt or they may slant. They may be mitered at the corners or they may be butt-jointed. But any block or border design that you can strip-piece can be used for a border. (Fig. 66-70)

In fact, blocks of many kinds can be used for

borders. (Fig. 71-74) Stars, Pinwheels, Four-Patches and other simple blocks are frequently used on old quilts. Mary Schafer is an expert at transforming a block design into a border design, and several of her best are shown here: FOX and GEESE, LINDEN MILL, NORTH CAROLINA LILY, OAK LEAF and CHERRIES and SINGLE CHAIN and KNOT. No matter what your pieced block design is, you can use all or part of it in an original border design. You will probably be able to use the same templates, or some of them at least, making your work easier and ensuring a harmony between block and border.

Other pieced designs such as BABY BLOCKS or BRAID have been used by many quilters in the past and are fairly popular still. (Fig. 75, 76)

Applique borders are most often used for applique block patterns, whether or not they contain elements from the blocks. While we do not think a pieced pattern necessarily calls for a pieced border instead of an applique border, keeping the techniques separate is the most common system. TOBACCO LEAF and KITE'S TAIL are two exceptions to the rule, showing once again that the only rules you **must** follow are your own. In our studies of old quilts, we have found many that used both techniques. In any case, the two kinds of borders are entirely different, with different strengths and weaknesses.

Applique borders are much more flexible and forgiving than pieced, so they are often easier to design and construct. They offer great potential for individual expression, but, because applique quilts are not popular in our quilt revival and because applique borders are infrequently used on pieced quilts, they have almost become extinct in this century. For examples of applique borders in all their variety and profusion, you must look at nineteenth century quilts. You will almost never find the same border twice, but there are only a few types: vines, swags and individual motif.

Vines are the most popular. Like vines in nature, vine borders sometimes have leaves, buds or flowers and sometimes bees or birds swoop down among the leaves, as they do on SUNBURST. The vines usually meander all the way around the quilt, but sometimes they stop at the corners or in the middle. Today most quilters are taught that the right way for borders to be made is symmetrical. That is, all four corners should match. Quilters of the past had other ideas. Meandering vines often wiggled aimlessly and naturally along, turning corners as they got to them. So one way to achieve the same "look" is to allow your applique border to direct itself.

Not all vine borders are asymmetrical, however. Many are perfectly planned and developed. Most of the examples in this book are very carefully worked out. Some travel continuously around the quilt, some are broken. Some have leaves, some have only flowers or buds.

The next most common applique border is the swag type. Like vines, swags come in many shapes and sizes, in all degrees of formality and artfulness. The intended effect of swag borders has almost always been to create a "regal," luxurious frame for a quilt, whether or not the effect is realized. Some swag designs are quite realistic, looking much like the draped fabric and ribbons they are supposed to represent. But most are fairly abstract, looking more like cut paper than draped fabric.

Swags are even easier to design than vines and show the creativity of traditional quilters in details, rather than overall concepts. Some have scalloped edges, some smooth; some are made of one fabric only, others of two or three; some have tassels, others have bows, still others have nothing at the points. With all these options, swags can range from very light and delicate, like those on COUNTRYSIDE, to very dense and heavy, like those on COXCOMB.

Among our favorite applique borders are the **individual motif** designs: the trees, baskets, pots of flowers and other pictorial designs that are scattered around some borders. Quilters have been wildly imaginative with these kinds of borders, taking advantage of the flexibility of applique to the fullest. There are no "typical" motifs, as all these borders were original ideas, seemingly invented for each quilt. They range from realistic pictures of trees or flowerpots to completely abstract shapes that seem to be of organic origin. DOUBLE PYRAMID and SUNFLOWER are two good examples.

If you decide to use this kind of border on your quilt, you may want to use similar organic motifs, or you may want to design your own geometric shape, your own picture or your own basket. Weeping Willow trees, people, birds and butterflies have all graced quilts in the past.

Adding The Border

As with all aspects of quiltmaking, there are many possible ways to plan and construct the border for your quilt. Some authorities tell you to plan the borders at the same time that you plan the quilt. Usually the complete quilt is worked out on graph paper. This takes a lot of the guess work out of quiltmaking. Problems are identified and solved before construction begins.

Some quilters suggest designing the border first and then filling in the interior of the quilt. Again, everything is worked out on graph paper first.

Some quiltmakers prefer to complete the interior of the quilt before they make the final decision about the border. This is the way most of our quilts were made. While we generally have a pretty good idea about the border design, we like to reserve final judgment until the interior of the quilt is finished. Discussions about possible border treatments continue through the construction process and upon completion we like to take a few days to reassess earlier ideas and consider new possibilities. We hang it on the wall and look at it that way or we lay it on the floor and play with color and dimension.

All of these methods are legitimate; which one to use is simply a matter of personal choice. Our point here is that it is important to select the method which seems the most natural and works the best for you. It never hurts to read all the "how-to" instructions you can—the more you know, the more choices you have.

Two problems you may have with borders are getting opposite borders the same size and getting the borders to lay flat without ruffling. Here are a few ideas which will help you avoid these problems as you add the borders.

If you plan your quilt on graph paper completely, you will know what size to cut the borders. People who use this method suggest cutting the borders to the size specified in the original drawing and fitting the quilt interior to the border as a way to make sure they fit correctly and lay flat.

If you make the quilt interior without working it out on paper first, you will have to rely on measuring the top to get the border size. If the top is heavily pieced it is sometimes difficult to measure. To get the most accurate measurement, press the quilt top (gently, without stretching it), and lay it flat on the floor, completely smoothed out. Compare the measurements of the opposite sides to see if there are any discrepencies. If the measurements differ by ¾ inch or less, you can make the borders a compromise length. Also, when you are adding a 90″ border to a pieced interior, it is quite possible that you could miss by a ¼″ or so. Thus, it is sometimes safer to place a pin at the correct measurement and cut the border a little longer.

Careful pinning can save trouble later. One way to do this is to measure and mark the border to correspond with the block size so they can be lined up and pinned. Another approach is to divide both the top and the border into fourths, pin these first and then pin the remainder to fit.

A common approach today, although rarely used in the past, is to sew four long borders on and let the corners lap over each other, then fold the top one diagonally from the inside corner out and hand stitch it to the bottom one. This produces a mitered corner, which some insist on and others never use.

If you are adding straight whole cloth borders you can add the sides first and then the top and bottom like this. (A)

Some borders are made using the carpenter method. (B) Here the borders are added going around the quilt in one direction, first the top, then the right side, then the bottom and finally the left side.

If your border has corner squares you can either use the carpenter method or you can use the method shown here. (C) The sides are added first, then the corner squares are sewn onto the top and bottom borders at both ends and added to the quilt.

If you want the borders on your quilt to work out symmetrically at the corners there are a number of general principles which apply to both pieced and applique borders.

Because of the nature of fabric, it is almost always necessary to make tiny adjustments to make a pieced or applique border work out exactly. With a little planning, however, you can minimize the discrepencies.

Begin by determining the length of the borders, minus the corner units as shown. (D) Second, determine the unit size. By "unit size" we mean the repeat length of the design, such as one swag in a swag border. If you select a unit length that will divide evenly into both borders, then all the corners will be symmetrical. If you can't come up with a unit size that works for both the length and the width you have at least five options.

The old-fashioned treatment is to ignore the corners and simply run the design to the end of the border and stop, as the quilter did on LOVE APPLE. A second idea is to design the corners to work out the same and create a resolution in the middle by adding to or subtracting from the pattern, or even introducing a new design. LINDEN MILL and SINGLE CHAIN and KNOT make subtle and effective use of this idea. A third technique is to make a number of tiny adjustments to either lengthen or shorten the unit size as needed. In the case of applique vine borders, a fourth idea is to let the vine begin and end anywhere and introduce another design in the four corners, as we did on KITE'S TAIL. The fifth method is to settle for opposite corners that are the same. This is seen frequently on Sawtooth borders.

Vine borders are easy to manipulate. Corners can be worked out first and the unit size is easy to adjust, as the vine is totally flexible.

Swag borders present few engineering problems because they can easily be adjusted to fit and the corner swag can be designed last to accomodate the side borders. (F, G) Note in these two examples that the side swags enter the corners at a different place and the corner swags are designed to fit.

Even with careful planning, a heavily pieced border may not always fit exactly when added to the body of the quilt. Pieced borders which have many seams can have a lot of give. They can therefore be stretched just a little or the fullness can be eased in to fit. This is a principle common to all sewing. Another solution is to make a number of tiny adjustments. If you are adding a sawtooth border, for example, and you end up half a triangle too long, simply take a tiny bit larger seam on 6 or 8 or 10 triangles and reduce the length of the border inconspicuously.

Another method is to just make up the sawtooth strip without any planning for size and make it fit with the gradual tiny adjustment system just described. The double sawtooth border on our full-size blue and white SAVANNAH STAR was made in this way. This sytem will almost always work with small triangles.

Another technique is to design all four corners the

same and make any neccessary adjustments in the middle of the border. If the pattern is a small repeat, the adjust can probably be made by taking a larger seam in a number of the units. If the pattern is a large repeat, this is not always possible. Then it may be necessary to introduce a new design element in the middle.

To make strip-pieced borders, long bands of fabric are sewn together and then cut to the width of the border and sewn together as shown. (H, I) For making diagonal borders, such as the one on JOSEPH'S COAT, the strips are staggered to save fabric. Strip borders are made with either equal width or different width strips.

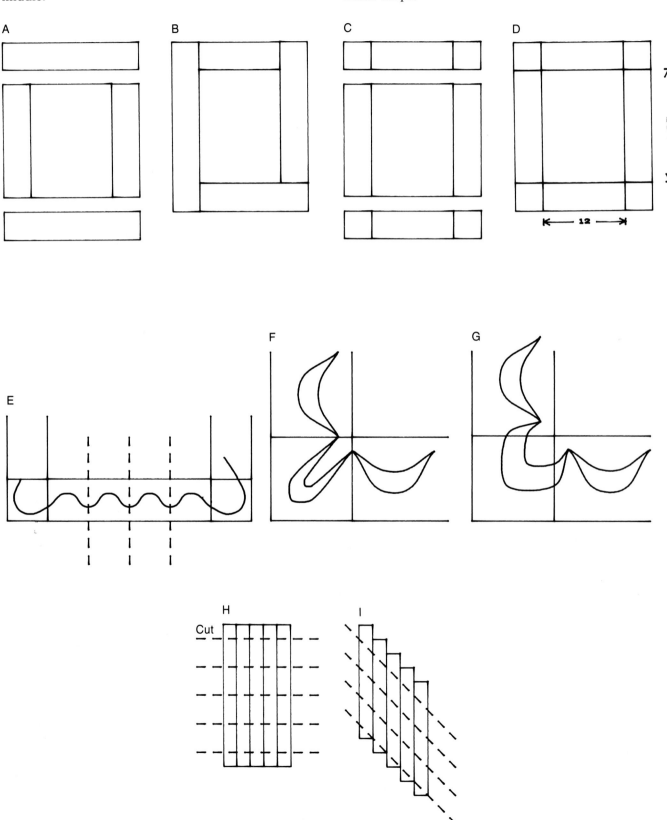

Gallery of Quilts

BIRDS IN FLIGHT. 72″ x 72″, 1984. Made by the authors. Cotton; polyester batting.

While this quilt has a very modern feeling, it was designed and made with all traditional "tools." The block is a common one, but the set is unusual in that there are two colors of plain blocks and fewer pieced ones than usual. Our idea was to stay close to the tradition and achieve a contemporary design.

Set: The set is on the straight with asymmetrical plain blocks. By flipping some of the blocks and changing the color of the large triangles to match the adjacent plain blocks, we found that it seemed not to be made of blocks. Instead, it seems like two large areas, one black and one white, with bits of color set in.

Border: Some quilts do not seem to call for a border, and this is one.

BLACK ELEGANCE. 80½″ x 98″, 1979.
Made by Mary Schafer.
Cotton; polyester batting.

Mary was inspired to make this quilt after seeing a tiny picture of one quilt block in a magazine. It is unusual among new quilts in that it is a two-color quilt, black and white. In fact, this is a fine example of what we think of as the "Mary Schafer Treatment" for quilt design: room for quilting between blocks, original border and impeccable engineering.

Set: The blocks are set on the diagonal with alternate plain blocks. Notice the unique quilting design in the plain blocks, designed just for this quilt.

Border: The Zig-Zag border would not be effective without the dark band framing it. The corner resolution is original, like most aspects of this quilt, and is only one of the many ways this corner could be handled. Mary used another border like this on Grandmother's Pride—see how she treats the corner there.

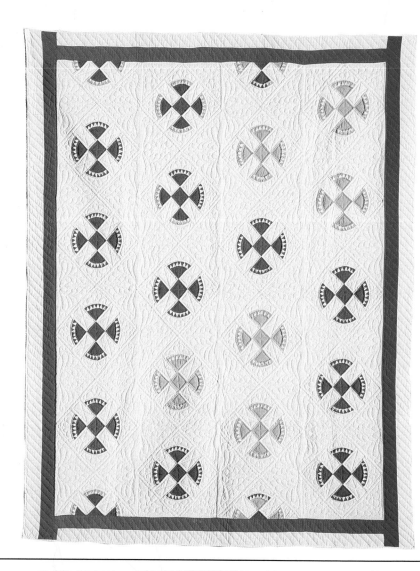

CIRCULAR SAW. 65″ x 83″,
top ca. 1900. Completed by
authors in 1985.
Cotton; polyester batting.

We found this quilt top in Burlington, Iowa, and were intrigued with the red and tan color scheme. How should we quilt it? Where did the scraps come from? Why was it never finished?

Set: Even though we almost never see this set in quilt books or magazines, we have seen quite a few in the field. We call it the Streak of Lightning set. (see pg. 14) It is constructed by setting the blocks on the diagonal in columns, with every other column starting with a half-block. Because of the technique, we think of it as a Bars Set variation.

Border: The interrupted border is another old-fashioned element of the Circular Saw. The top and bottom borders were finished before the side borders were put on. We treated the border strips as one when it came to the quilting, putting simple diagonals across both.

CHERRY BASKET. 72″ x 84″, ca. 1900. Made by Lucy Ann Brown of Paris, KY. Cotton; cotton batting. Collected by the authors.

We feel that this Afro-American quilt is one of the most exciting in our collection. It has several aspects that intrigue us. First, every other pieced block is pieced of white-on-white fabric! We have examined the seams in minute detail, but can find no trace of color ever having been there. Second, the border is unusual, to say the least. And, third, the quilting of freehand wavy lines is just like we have seen on other Afro-American quilts, leading us to think there may have been a technique or style we hope to learn more about.

Set: The blocks are set on the diagonal either alternate plain blocks **and** alternate pieced blocks. The cherries in all blocks are appliqued with a buttonhole stitch over raw edges, with red thread for the red cherries, white thread for the white.

Border: Two white bands of equal width, with red inserts in the inner corners. We think Mrs. Brown might have run low on red fabric and designed the whole quilt to use up what she had. The backing has been brought around one-half inch and sewn down for the binding.

CHERRY BASKET. 47″ x 39¾″, 1985. Made by Mary Schafer. Cotton & cotton sateen; polyester batting.

When Mary saw our Cherry Basket, she did what she usually does when she is very moved by something—she made a quilt. Hers, though, shows her personality just as surely as Lucy Ann Brown's. Mary used white sateen for the white-on-white work, and appliqued the cherries with a whip stitch. The quilting, too, is all Mary: original cherry wreaths. Overall, it is a fine tribute to an earlier quiltmaker.

CLAMSHELL. 79″ x 97½″, 1966. Made by Mary Schafer. Cotton; polyester batting.

This is an unusual quilt by any standards. Technically, it is one of the most demanding ever devised, with every single seam being pieced on the curve. Also, it was probably the first Clamshell of modern times, certainly the first ever to use the printed fabrics in such an innovative way. It received two blue ribbons at the first NQA show in 1971: Best Pieced Quilt and Viewer's Choice.

Set: While the Clamshell is an all-over one-patch pattern, here Mary has arranged the colors to make a medallion. Nearly every print is mirrored right to left as well as vertically, creating an artful, understated symmetry.

Border: The borders are created only with color. This is one of Mary's cleverest border ideas ever, and one which could work with virtually any one-patch pattern.

**COUNTRYSIDE. 80″ x 86″, 1980. Made by Mary Schafer.
Cotton & cotton chintz; polyester batting.**

(The quilt which inspired this one is pictured in *Quilts in America* on page 97. It was made in New England in 1813.)

We have come to think that medallion quilts have a certain "look" that is actually a modern creation. Early medallions were tremendously varied and much different from contemporary ones. This one was named by Mary for the center panel of fabric, which shows scenes taken from rural life.

Set: This medallion set, open and airy, is the opposite of many medallions. Instead of being built around a showy center block, it is built around a twenty-four-inch square piece of whole cloth.

Border: The borders are all made in two-inch increments. The first pieced border is four inches wide. The next is four inches on the side, six on the top and bottom. The next four borders are two inches each, and the outside one is twelve.

The inside applique is what is called "broderie perse," or pictures cut out of one fabric and laid onto another—in this case the pictures are of flowers, but birds, bugs and all kinds of plants are common as well.

The outside applique swags have an embroidered line and bow of black crewelwork thread.

**COXCOMB. 73″ x 80″, 1984.
Made by the authors.
Cotton; polyester batting.**

This original design was derived by folding and cutting paper—snowflake style—to make a block pattern in the style of some of the fine old appliques. As it seemed a little "heavy" when the applique was done, we used reverse applique to lighten the large red areas. In keeping with the old style we used red and green, even though it is hard for most people to see that color combination without thinking "Christmas.".

Set: Of course this is a four-block set. This version is a little odd because it has lattice strips between the blocks. We added the applique in the center because it seemed empty without it.

Border: The swag design was derived the same way as the block design, by folding and cutting paper. The scalloped, two-color swags seem to carry on the flamboyant theme of the blocks.

CHURN DASH. 79″ x 96″, 1982.
Made by Mary Schafer. Cotton; polyester batting.

The placement of the fabrics in this scrap quilt is highly organized. Stylistically, it resembles the scrap quilts made of shirtings around the turn of this century.

Set: The blocks are set on the diagonal with alternate plain blocks. The familiar Churn Dash block looks more like a lantern when it is set this way. Note the careful repetition of the colors and how it gives the design a subtle cohesion.

Border: This is the same motif Gwen used on Flying Swallows, and once again the fabrics are carefully repeated. The outside border dimensions were not determined by visual considerations, but by the size of the bed.

CHURN DASH. 79″ x 88½″, top ca. 1915.
Completed by Mary Schafer.
Cotton; cotton batting.

Set: The blocks are set in bars with lavender plain blocks between the pieced ones. The whole-cloth bars are two inches wider than the blocks, perhaps to emphasize the set. Also, the bars of pieced blocks are staggered—one starting with a pieced block, the next with a plain.

Border: A plain inner border surrounds the blocks. Mary added the outer border to "bring it out to size."

DOUBLE PYRAMID. 67½″ x 81½″, 1850-1875. Made by Martha Wade Sherwood of Holly, Michigan. Collected by Mary Schafer. Cotton; cotton batting.

Mrs. Sherwood was the wife of a dairy farmer and, judging from this example, a very good quiltmaker. The applique border helps give this quilt a light-hearted charm. Although the block pattern is difficult, the quilt retains an effortless feeling.

Set: The blocks are set diagonally with alternate plain blocks.

Border: This individual applique motif could be a simplified fleur-de-lis or a stylized flower. Because the shapes are irregular and inconsistently placed, we think they were cut freehand from the fabric, with no pattern, and placed only by eye, with no measurements.

ENGLISH PLUME. 80½″ x 97″, 1967-1972. Made by Elizabeth Harriman & Mary Schafer. Cotton; polyester batting.

This could be called the "One Block" set, or we could think of it as a simple medallion. In any case, it is the same type of quilt design as the Lone Star. It is remarkable for its scale—the largest applique block outside Hawaii.

Set: The single large block has a reverse applique star in the middle and reverse applique lines in the middle of each plume.

Border: These leaves seem to be sewn down where they fell. Each one has an applique spine. The design is one of the most naturalistic of all. The borders are wider at the top and bottom to make the square design into a rectangular quilt.

FEATHER-EDGED STAR. 77″ x 97″, 1984. Made by Mary Schafer. Cotton; polyester batting.

The briefest look tells us that this scrap quilt was made by a master of quiltmaking. It is beautifully composed and perfectly made. The fabrics are carefully arranged, the quilting is unusually rich and the applique border makes a great frame.

Set: The twelve pieced stars are set on the diagonal with alternate plain blocks which have been heavily quilted.

Border: It has become a convention of modern quiltmaking that a pieced quilt gets a pieced border and an applique quilt an applique border. It is a convention, not a law. The two kinds of borders have many uses that have been little explored. Even though the design of this vine border contains no elements of the block design, the two complement each other and work together well, partly because the colors in the blocks all reappear in the border.

FLOWERING ALMOND. 83″ x 97″, 1968-1971. Made by Elizabeth Harriman & Mary Schafer. Cotton; polyester batting.

We have seen a number of variations of this pattern, and know others with this name. It is a strange pattern, often fairly crudely executed. This one is uniquely light and graceful.

Set: The large blocks—twenty-three-inches square—are set on the straight, block to block. The wide white margin around the applique on each block creates a sort of lattice between the designs.

Border: Surely one of the most abstract applique borders of all time, this individual motif design has a clever resolution in the middle of each side. It does seem to "relate" to the block design, but it is hard to imagine the designer's source of inspiration for it.

FLYING SWALLOWS.
78″ x 90″, 1981. Made by the authors. Cotton; polyester batting.

The light blue blocks were made from Joe's Egyptian cotton shirt that he washed with an ink pen in the pocket after the first wearing. Gwen tried to turn a sad experience into a glad one by secretly making this quilt top for him for his birthday. It became the first in a series of birthday quilt tops she continues to make for him to quilt.

Set: The blocks are set on the straight with lattice strips and contrasting corner squares.

Border: The wide border has an individual motif design across each end. (from *American Quilts and How To Make Them*, p. 183) The quilting lines were a result of our ongoing study of mattress pads and other machine-quilted items—simple diagonal lines that become interesting if properly used.

FLOWER POT. 30″ x 37″, 1983. Made by the authors. Cotton; cotton flannel batting.

We have always been fascinated with the bold, bright folk designs of the Pennsylvania Germans, and this original design crib quilt was an attempt to work in that style. The stems are made of antique, hand-woven tape. The quilting designs were drawn freehand.

Set: This is the one-block, or "pictorial" set. It is a kind of simplified medallion.

Border: This spiky sawtooth variation seemed like a good way to enclose the bold, oversized flower pot. It is made of an elongated right triangle. Because it is large in proportion to the middle of the quilt, and because of its strong color contrast, it has an almost explosive energy.

FOUR PATCH. 82″ x 88″, 1979. Made by the authors. Cotton; polyester batting.

FOUR PATCH reflects our early infatuation with the Amish style. Other than the printed fabric triangles in the bars, this is similar to many Amish quilts.

Set: This is a straightforward Bars set. The blocks are set on the diagonal with alternate plain bars.

Border: We borrowed the standard Amish format of narrow inner border and wide outer border. Our idea was to work with simple, uncomplicated line and form.

FOUR PATCH. 33″ x 39½″, 1981. Made by the authors. Cotton; polyester batting.

This quilt was inspired by one in *A Gallery of Amish Quilts*, a rare Amish crib quilt.

Set: Even a simple four-patch becomes hard to identify when it is set together block-to-block like this. It seems more like a one-patch. While the intent of the quiltmaker was no doubt much different, the effect of the quilt is similar to some paintings by Paul Klee.

Border: One advantage of this common border type is its flexible dimensions. They can be altered to make the quilt exactly the size you want.

FOUR PATCH. 69″ x 83″, 1985. Made by the authors. Cotton; one-half Fairfield Cotton Classic batting.

As we have never found a name for this four-patch variation we usually call it, "Big and Little." We got the idea for this quilt from an antique top we saw during a Show-and-Tell segment of a guild meeting.

Set: The design relies on the block-to-block set. Two different four-patch blocks alternate in the straight and the colors run diagonally across the quilt.

Border: In keeping with the scrap quilt sensibility of the blocks, we used typical scrap quilt border techniques. The sides were finished before we put the end borders on. When we ran out of the red print we were using, we substituted another. Once again, it is from old quilts that we get our ideas, and it is the quilts that look like this which we enjoy the most.

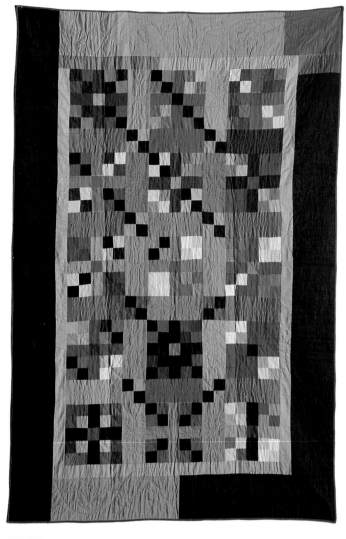

FOUR PATCH or CROSS IN THE SQUARE. 48″ x 72″, 1985. Made by the authors. Cotton & cotton sateen; one-half Fairfield Cotton Classic batting.

Gwen made this top for Joe's birthday in 1984. It incorporates many of our favorite Midwest Amish scrap quilting concepts, including its dimensions. Quilts this size were often made for the small cots that the hired hands slept on—so we call this a "hired hand's" quilt.

Set: The fifteen blocks are set on the straight with lattice strips made of scraps. When the lattice is made of the same fabrics as the blocks, it seems to be almost a part of the block design.

Border: Four colors in the outer border and two greys in the inner one convey the idea that this is a real scrap quilt, using whatever fabrics were available.

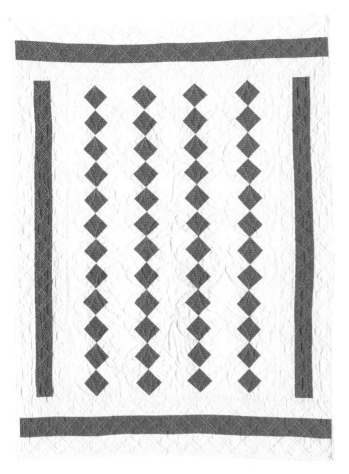

FOUR PATCH CHAIN. 25″ x 33″, 1985. Made by the authors. Cotton; cotton batting.

Many of our quilts are made to illustrate our lectures. This little crib quilt was a test piece for a cotton batting, but since we had to make **some** kind of top, we made our favorite two-color type and quilted it with a teacup design.

Set: This is the same block pattern we used for Kite's Tail, but set on the diagonal instead of the straight. As with Kite's Tail, the colored squares are all you see. The quilting, too, helps to mask the piecing lines.

Border: This is a prime example of the "interrupted" border.

FOX AND GEESE. 78″ x 90″, 1964. Made by Mary Schafer. Cotton; polyester batting.

With its color scheme taken from the fox and its clever border design, this quilt shows how original and witty a simple pieced quilt can be.

Set: The pieced blocks are set on the diagonal with alternate plain blocks. Set like this, it has a vague resemblance to Zuni or Hopi sand paintings.

Border: Beyond the wide, white inner border is the pieced border and a narrow outer band. The pieced design comes directly from the block.

GRAPES AND VINES. 83½" x 97", 1972. Made by Mary Schafer. Cotton; polyester batting.

In the first quilt book of this century, *Quilts: Their Story and How to Make Them*, (1915) Marie Webster showed an original design for which she sold the pattern. Many years later Mary acquired the pattern and made this version of Grapes and Vines. The original must have been one of the finest quilts of this century, as well as a great example of the influence of the Art and Craft movement on quilt design—proof of Marie Webster's sophisticated aesthetics.

Set: Of course this is a four-block set, and the only one in this book with appliqued lattice between the blocks. The lattice applique uses motifs from the block, but, like the border, it is a separate design.

Border: The elegant border pattern derives much of its effect from the yards and yards of twining and curling bias tape. The combination of the hundreds of oval grapes and yards of bias makes this one of the most difficult of all patterns.

GRANDMOTHER'S PRIDE. 79″ x 99″, 1980. Made by Mary Schafer. Cotton; polyester batting.

Inspired by a magazine article on classic fan designs, Mary made this Art Deco-inspired pattern with the pastels so popular during the thirties.

Set: When these nine-inch blocks are set on the diagonal like this, they look as much like flower pots as fans. The blocks are separated by a three-inch lattice.

Border: Outside the beautifully quilted inner border, the Zig-Zag makes a fine frame for the blocks. A more common way to use the pattern would have been to make the zig-zag of the printed fabric and to use white for the background. Here it is reversed. Note the original corner resolution, one of countless possible corner treatments.

JACOB'S LADDER VARIATION. 64″ x 77″, 1985. Made by the authors. Cotton; one-half Fairfield Cotton Classic batting.

In our travels we have met many people who say they are insecure about choosing colors for their quilts. Since some of the finest quilts ever made used red and white only, or indigo blue and white, we feel that one way to avoid the problem is to make this kind of quilt—which happens to be one of our very favorites. Of course, they are not too popular during this revival, but were enormously so in the past.

Set: This is a nine-patch type of block, set block-to-block on the straight. There could be no better illustration of our points about the block-to-block set: it obscures the block design and it creates new patterns where the blocks meet.

Border: There seemed to be plenty of action in the interior of the quilt, so we decided to add only a simple whole-cloth band. We marked and quilted the cable in the old style as well—without corner resolutions.

THE HARVESTERS. 82″ x 97½″, 1980. Made by Mary Schafer. Cotton; polyester batting.

This quilt was named for the small center panel of fabric that shows a group of people harvesting wheat. It is an imitation of the Early American medallions which were often made of scraps, an **informal** rather than a formal medallion. Nevertheless, the fabrics are not placed at random, but arranged according to a scheme.

Set: A classic medallion.

Border: This quilt consists of almost nothing but borders. They are all either sawtooth variations or squares. Perhaps because of the fabric placement, it never seems chaotic or uncontrolled, only lush. The borders were all designed on a two-inch scale, that is, they are all multiples of two inches, so the corners all resolve neatly.

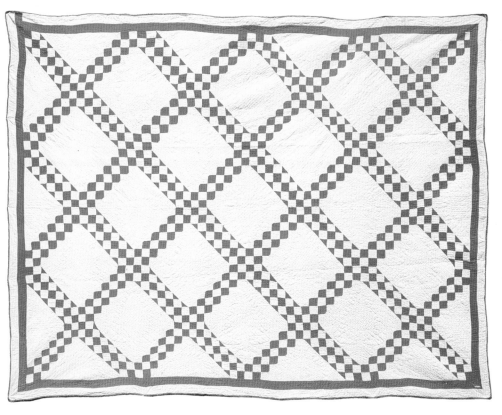

IRISH CHAIN VARIATION.
60″ x 83″, ca. 1875-1900. Collected
by the authors in Flint, Michigan.
Cotton; cotton batting.

We call this an Irish Chain variation even though it has little in common with that pattern. Where Irish Chains are made of pieced blocks set with plain blocks, this design is made of pieced lattice strips that have plain blocks set in the spaces. It is beautifully made and has tiny quilting stitches. The batting is a very thin layer of cotton with many seeds in it, so thin that it is hard to see the elaborate pineapples quilted into the plain blocks.

Set: This all-over set is made of lattice stripping. Notice the color reversal at the intersections.

Border: The border is made of two equal bands, quilted with triple diagonal lines and bound with a narrow, red strip cut on the straight and machine topstitched. We have always wondered why the quiltmaker chose to run one red band all the way to the edge.

JOSEPH'S COAT. 77″ x 80″, 1920.
Made by Sarah Gruber Retlogle,
Breezewood, Pennsylvania. Cotton; cotton
batting. Collected by the authors.

Sarah was a farmer's wife, originally a Dunkard, who later converted to the Mennonite faith. Her JOSEPH'S COAT is one of the finest we have ever seen, very closely quilted with a different motif for each color.

Set: This is a form of the Bars design that seems to have been popular mostly among Mennonites. It's format is a simplified medallion.

Border: This strip border may have been strip-pieced. It is quilted with a diamond pattern.

JULIANA. 79″ x 88½″, 1985. Made by Mary Schafer. Cotton; polyester batting.

Mary named this quilt after her mother, Juliana Zelko Vida, who died of tuberculosis at the age of twenty-six. Unusual color gives it a fittingly somber air.

Set: The blocks are set on the diagonal with alternate plain blocks. The plain blocks are quilted with an original floral wreath design.

Border: While the border design seems fairly simple, it is meticulously planned and executed. The isosceles triangle pieced border is framed with a five-inch brown band. The next two borders measure two and three inches—together the same width as the brown band.

KITE'S TAIL. 68½″ x 85″, 1984. Made by the authors. Cotton; Fairfield Cotton Classic batting.

This blue and white quilt is like many made in the nineteenth century: economical of design and technique and effective in a quiet way.

Set: We started work on this quilt with a very simple idea—a simple four-patch and a simple, straight set could make an interesting quilt. The alternate plain block arrangement is interrupted at one end with a row of blocks set on their points.

Border: The border design was taken directly from a quilt made in 1778 in Lancaster, Pennsylvania. (Hall and Kretzinger, p. 180) The lively vine is as uncontrolled as the interior is subdued. The contrast itself was what made us want to use it.

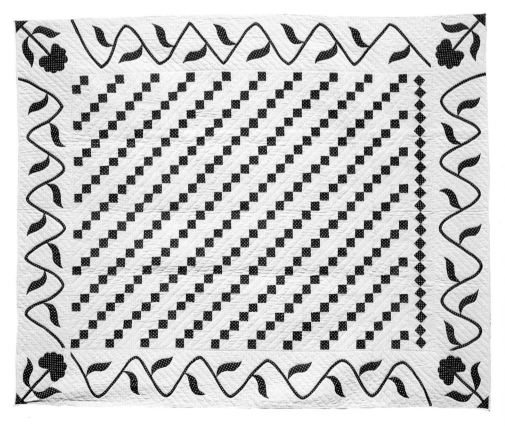

LINDEN MILL. 80" x 96", 1980.
Made by Mary Schafer. Cotton; polyester batting.

One of the best features of this quilt is its clever solution to the problem of running out of fabric. When Mary saw she was not going to have enough of the print to finish the blocks and the border, she introduced a plain blue fabric in six of the outer blocks and the border.

Set: The blocks are set on the diagonal with alternate plain blocks.

Border: With white borders on both sides of the pieced border, and with so much white in it as well, the pieced border ends up resembling small, blue creatures making their way around the corners and meeting in the middle of each side. All its components come from the block pattern.

LOBSTER. 77" x 93", 1969. Made by Mary Schafer. Cotton; polyester batting.

This is one of only two known quilts of this pattern. In Florence Peto's book, *Historic Quilts*, there is a photograph of a Lobster quilt of this pattern, together with the description of how it was machine-appliqued and machine-quilted **block by block** and assembled after all the blocks were complete. This version was made entirely by hand. When Mrs. Peto learned that Mary had made this Lobster, she wrote to tell her how pleased she was.

Set: The blocks are set block-to-block on the straight. Some of the pincers were left off the corners of some blocks to vary the design. Diagonal quilting lines tie the blocks together in yet another way.

Border: The wide white border has an applique design that could be titled: "Pinchers Over the Waves." It is an artful and understated complement to the almost threatening interior.

LOG CABIN, BARN RAISING. 74″ x 74″, 1984. Made by the authors. Cotton & cotton sateen; Fairfield Cotton Classic batting.

This, another of Gwen's birthday quilts for Joe, is a log cabin quilt done primarily with scraps left over from making Amish-style quilts. We have heard many times that traditional quiltmakers would sometimes include a deliberate imperfection to avoid competing with the Creator, who alone should be perfect. Perhaps they did. In our experience, it has never been necessary to make **deliberate** mistakes. The mis-set block at the edge of this quilt simply went unnoticed until the quilt was in the frame.

Set: BARN RAISING, according to our studies, is probably the most popular of the log cabin sets. Its effect is like that of a mandala, to which it is similar.

Border: About one-half of the antique log cabin quilts we have seen have no border. In a way, no border is a type of border — this type.

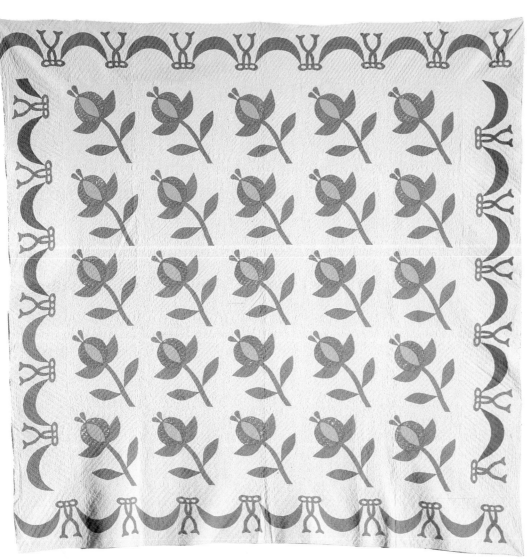

LOVE APPLE. 87″ x 88½″, ca. 1850. Signed in ¼″ tall cross stitch: "Miss Susannah Allen." Collected by Mary Schafer in Gettysburg, Pennsylvania. Cotton; cotton batting.

Love Apple has all the best features of mid-nineteenth century applique work: red and green with a touch of mustard yellow for accent, exquisite workmanship and eccentric design.

Set: The blocks are set block-to-block, on the straight — a demonstration of the principle that beautiful blocks often need no fancy set.

Border: The applique on the four border panels was probably finished before the panels were attached to the quilt top, which would account for the corner treatment. Here, in a sort of bylaw of the famous Bauhaus' concept that "Form Follows Function," — technique determines design.

MAY BASKET. 68″ x 82″, 1984. Made by the authors. Cotton; polyester batting.

We made this quilt to show the importance of quilting designs on a quilt that has room for them. Without the elaborate quilting, this quilt would seem modest to the point of being dull.

Set: The basket blocks are set on the diagonal with alternate plain blocks, leaving room for quilting and emphasizing the individual blocks.

Border: We treated the red and white bands as one border by quilting triple diagonals across both. Once again, simple multiple bands can make a fine border.

NINE PATCH. 60″ x 78″, 1986. Quilt top made by the authors. Cotton.

Two of the quilts in this book use the Streak of Lightning set, but neither uses a contrasting color like this for the "streak." We made this top one day while we were working on the manuscript and realized that we needed an example.

Set: Our favorite aspect of this kind of set is its optical illusion effect—looked at one way the blocks seem to be in the foreground; in another, they seem to recede behind the red zig-zags.

Border: When we finish this quilt, we will leave it like this — with no border.

NINE PATCH. 80″ x 88″, 1982. Made by the authors. Cotton; polyester batting.

This Amish-style nine-patch is fairly representative of the Lancaster County style: wide borders, simple design, large-scale feather quilting.

Set: The blocks are set diagonally with alternate plain blocks. Note the extra green block in one corner, which we included when we happened to reach that end of the quilt with an extra green and no red blocks. When necessity played a larger part in quiltmaking than it does today, many stray blocks and fabrics found their way into quilts.

Border: The inner border is a Streak of Lightning pattern like that shown in Figure 59. We made no attempt to coordinate it with the interior. Instead, we decided to introduce the jarring and intense turquoise. Sometimes we have looked at this quilt and felt that the rest of it existed as a ground for the Streak of Lightning border!

The wide black border provides a perfect area for heavy quilting.

NORTH CAROLINA LILY. 78″ x 94″, 1971. Made by Mary Schafer. Cotton; polyester batting.

This is one of the most "refined" of the patterns called "North Carolina Lily." When it is combined with such fine quilting and beautiful border design, it makes a rare and handsome quilt.

Set: The blocks are designed to be set on the diagonal, as these are. But, instead of being arranged all one way, these have been turned to look "right" from any direction. The alternate plain blocks are quilted with traditional feather wreaths.

Border: The original border design is surprisingly uncomplicated. A flower from the block has been grafted onto a wandering, leafy vine, with a bud tucked neatly into each corner.

OAK LEAF AND CHERRIES. 78″ x 99″, 1969. Made by Mary Schafer. Cotton; polyester batting.

This block pattern was published in Rose Wilder Lane's book *Needlework in America*. It is one of those that allude to American history without specific references.

Set: The blocks are set on the diagonal with alternate plain blocks. Set this way, the block's spare, light look is emphasized.

Border: The original border design is a rearrangement of the block parts along a continuous vine. As in the blocks, all the cherries are stuffed.

PIECED SAMPLERS. 77½″ x 93″, ca. 1850. Maker unknown, collected in Berks County, Pennsylvania. In the Shafer and Marston/Cunningham Collections.

These rare pieced samplers were once sewn together as the front and back of a slipcover, probably for a feather comforter. One side was mostly light, one was mostly dark. Even after Mary Schafer's extensive and careful repairs, they are extremely fragile.

Set: Blocks of many sizes and fabrics were sewn together randomly to make wild designs.

Border: Mary added the borders of plain bands to protect these fragile pieces.

PRAIRIE QUEEN. 82″ x 97″, 1985. Made by Mary Schafer. Cotton; polyester batting.

Pieced of striped, checked and plaid shirtings, Prairie Queen resembles quilts made in the last quarter of the last century. The browns, reds and blues are rarely used like this today.

Set: This Streak of Lightning set has two features which make it unlike most contemporary sets: first, it uses half blocks in the alternate rows and second, it begins with a half block on the left and ends with a full block on the right, a type of arrangement often called "unbalanced." We feel there is more to balance than starting and ending with the same thing. In fact, this quilt seems very well balanced.

Border: Two narrow inner borders and one wide outer border frame the blocks. Note the two delicate quilting designs on the white borders.

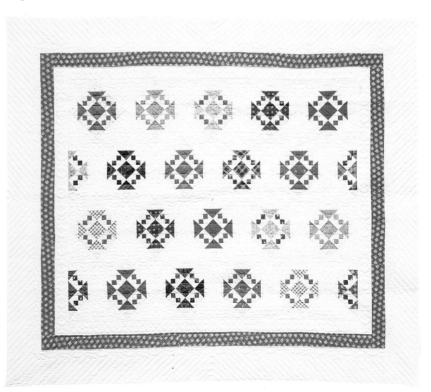

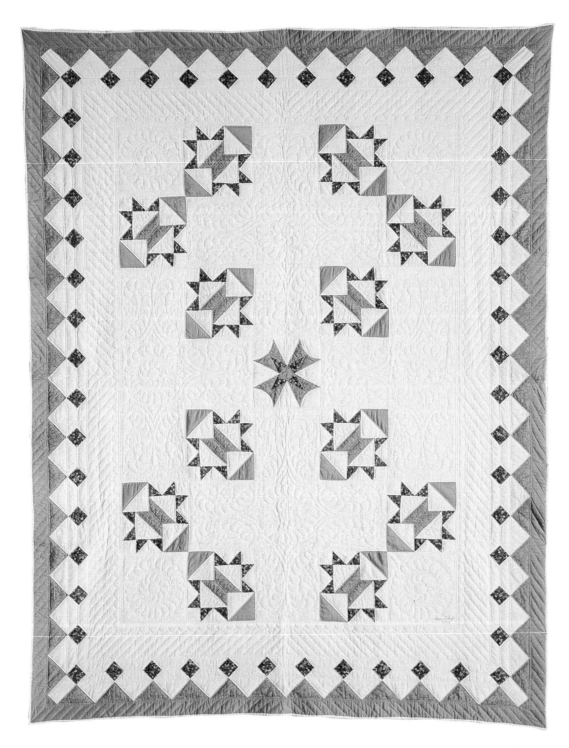

QUEEN CHARLOTTE'S CROWN. 76″ x 98″, 1973. Made by Mary Schafer. Cotton; polyester batting.

This quilt is a tribute to Queen Charlotte, this country's last queen. Therefore, all its parts were designed to evoke majesty and pomp. The maltese cross in the middle symbolizes King George III.

Set: The blocks are set on the straight with alternate plain blocks. Four pieced blocks were left out, to create rows of crowns, all pointing to King George. The large white areas have a repeated plume design quilted in.

Border: The original border was meant to resemble points on a crown, carrying on the theme of the blocks, if not the exact pattern.

SAVANNAH STAR. 81″ x 81″, ca. 1910-1920. Collected by Mary Schafer in Flint, Michigan. Cotton; cotton batting.

A description of this quilt sounds much like the quilt in Plate 44, but the two have little in common—save the block pattern. This antique is made of scraps, skillfully blended and balanced. It is quilted with diagonal lines and a pattern called, "Hanging Diamonds." With the alternate plain blocks being colored instead of white, the set has a different, heavier feel.

Set: Set on the diagonal with alternate plain blocks, these pieced blocks seem to recede behind the predominate pink squares.

Border: The border is made of two bands of equal width. This is one of the few antique quilts we have seen with mitered corner borders.

SAVANNAH STAR. 76½″ x 97″, 1970. Made by Mary Schafer. Cotton; polyester batting.

No better argument for the importance of sets and borders needs to be made than a comparison of this quilt with the one that inspired it in Plate #45. Using the same block and essentially the same colors, two quiltmakers produced quite different quilts. This one has an uptown elegance; the other one has a homey charm.

Set: The blocks are set on the diagonal with lattice strips one-half the width of the block. As the lattice is the same color as the background color of the blocks, the clay-rose stars seem to float over a continuous field. The strips are quilted with original feather variations.

Border: This original vine border is the sort of design upon which you expect to find flowers and leaves. This vine grows stars.

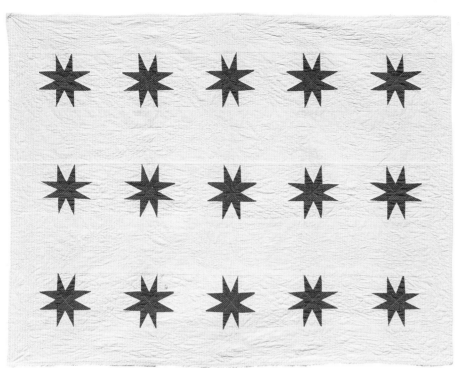

**SAVANNAH STAR. 34½″ x 42″, 1985.
Made by the authors. Cotton; one-half
Fairfield Cotton Classic batting.**

The block we used for illustration here
is made in simple blue and white, set together
in bars, all done primarily as a ground for
rich quilting designs we wanted to use.

Set: The blocks are set in bars with alternating plain strips one-half the height of the
block. Pieced bars alternate with plain bars
the same width.

Border: This simple, whole-cloth border
is heavily quilted with a freehand-drawn
original feather design.

**SAVANNAH STAR. 79″ x 92″, 1984.
Made by the authors. Cotton; polyester
batting.**

We think of this one as an All-American
quilt. The colors, the block-style construction,
the sawtooth borders and the feather quilting
are all typical of American quilts.

Set: The blocks are set on the diagonal
with alternate plain blocks, which are quilted
with the common feather wreath. A quilt set
this way calls for more elaborate quilting than
one set block-to-block or otherwise closely
pieced.

Border: Narrow sawtooth borders both
pointing the same way, both turning the corner the same way, set off the wide white
border. The running vine quilting design is an
old one that looks like seaweed or corn leaves.

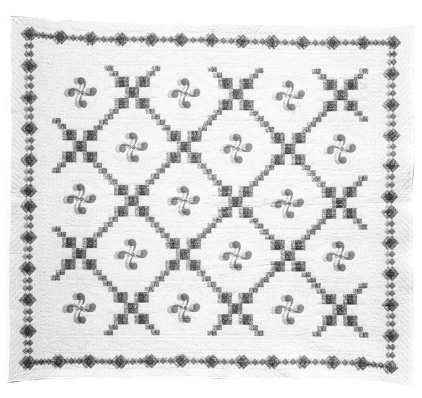

SINGLE CHAIN AND KNOT. 82½″ x 97″, 1974. Made by Mary Schafer. Cotton; polyester batting.

This is an original twist on a traditional pattern. The appliqued "knot" in the alternate blocks is taken from a Pennsylvania German design. Any quilt that has this much negative space calls for rich quilting, which this one has in abundance.

Set: The "chain" blocks are set on the straight with alternate applique blocks. You can imagine that the design seemed severely plain without the applique.

Border: The pieced border design uses both squares from the block pattern. It resolves cleverly in the middle of the top and bottom borders. With plain borders on each side, the brown squares make a chain to frame the quilt.

STAR AND CHERRIES. 29″ x 36″, 1984. Made by the authors. Cotton; one-half Fairfield Cotton Classic batting.

Being true scrap quilters, we hate to throw anything out. So when we had trouble piecing a star and had to start over, we saved the rejected pieces. (The star turned out fine.) One day we ran across the rejected ones and decided to make a quilt out of them which we could use during our lectures. This was the result. It has an unusual set, an applique border on a pieced quilt and unusual quilting designs. The clamshell quilting in the middle was marked with coins—some with a dime, some with a nickle.

Set: This is a variation of the one-block set.

Border: The original primitive applique pattern could be cherries, or it might be suckers or flowers. A feather quilting design follows the vine, using it as the "spine" of the feather.

SUNBURST. 80″ x 97″, 1980. Made by Mary Schafer. Cotton; polyester batting.

Something about quiltmaking is almost magical—the idea that an old dress and a worn out shirt can be transformed into such a glorious piece of work. This quilt evokes a picture of dawn, complete with birds flying from the vines that sheltered them for the night.

Set: The twenty pieced blocks are set together block-to-block on the straight. A quilting design in all four corners of each block meets to form a new design where the blocks come together.

Border: The colors and the flying birds make this convincing border perfect for the quilt. It is much more realistic than most vine designs.

SUNFLOWER, OR SUNBURST. 76½″ x 94″, ca. 1875. Collected by Mary Schafer in Macomb County, Michigan. Cotton; cotton batting.

This quilt has much in common with Double Pyramid. Both are two-color quilts from the same period and both have a lively, folk-art charm which expresses a confident, offhand creativity.

Set: The blocks are set block-to-block on the straight, with individual appliqued shapes at the corners. From the irregular shapes and placement, we think these shapes were cut freehand from the fabric, with no template, and laid on by eye, with no measurement.

Border: These abstract individual motif designs seem as spontaneous as it they were drawn. We do not know if they were meant only as shapes, or if they are supposed to be ram's horns, fluer-de-lis, leaves, flowers or anything else. In any case, they make a cheery border.

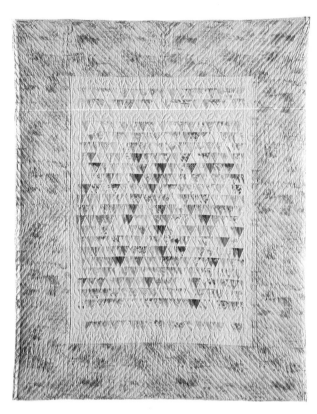

THOUSAND TRIANGLES. 66″ x 82″, 1983. Made by the authors. Cotton; cotton chintz; polyester batting.

We made this one-patch scrap quilt to explore the style of the early nineteenth-century scrap quilts. Just as common fabrics are sometimes elevated to lofty heights by their use in a quilt, so also can fine fabrics be used in everyday quilts, as we used them here.

Set: This is a one-patch design set in a simple medallion.

Border: The triangles are framed first by a beige strip, then a wide chintz border. Sometimes we include borders like this or other features not only because they are historically accurate for the style of the quilt, but also because they are out of fashion today.

TOBACCO LEAF. 79½″ x 96½″, 1977. Made by Mary Schafer. Cotton; polyester batting.

This pattern is rare among appliques for its refusal to be "pretty." It looks most like what it represents: a field of tobacco. According to Mary, the quilt was made to commemorate our country's first cash crop at the Jamestown settlement.

Set: The blocks are set block-to-block on the straight. The set and the quilting lines work together to make an extremely cohesive design.

Border: One could view the pieced section as several borders, but it is intended as a Tree of Life pattern, all one. It is a classic example of corner and middle resolutions. Any sawtooth design must change directions in the middle like this if it is to meet all four corners the same. The inner white border is quilted with a straight feather design, the outer with simple diagonals.

VARIABLE STAR. 34″ x 34″, 1981. Made by the authors. Cotton; polyester batting.

This exuberant little quilt was our first attempt in the Pennsylvania German style. All the fabrics are printed, and all are in colors typical of the style.

Set: The blocks are set on the straight with lattice strips between. The lattice has contrasting corner squares.

Border: The first border is a continuation of the sashing. The next, pieced border is a crazy sawtooth, with the colors and diagonal lines going in any direction. The yellow border is quilted with one-half inch diagonals.

WILD GOOSE CHASE. 84″ x 84″, 1981. Made by the authors. Cotton; polyester batting.

Our quilt was inspired by a crib quilt shown in the 1980 issue of *The Quilt Engagement Calender*, (Plate 45) (reprinted in *Treasury of American Quilts*, Plate 65.) It served a dual purpose for us. First, it helped us learn more about Pennsylvania German-style quilts, and second, it was a good project upon which Joe could learn applique. Ours is similar to the original, except full-size and with a large border.

Set: Most four-block quilts were applique, which was one reason we found this four-block pieced quilt exciting. A one and one-half-inch lattice separates the blocks and meets in the middle at four tiny triangles. The quilt block is actually the Wild Goose Chase block, but applique patterns have been added to it in an original way.

Border: The wide green border has a Wild Goose Chase border inserted in the middle, with triangles the same size as those in the block.

WASHINGTON PLUME. 93″ x 93″, 1968. Made by Mary Schafer. Cotton; polyester batting.

This quilt is squarely in the tradition of Early American medallions. It is a replica of a quilt presented to the Mt. Vernon Ladies Association in 1876, said to be very old even at that time. Perhaps its chief departure from the contemporary medallion style is that, while most contemporary medallions are made with carefully coordinated groups of colors, this derives its elegance from two colors only.

Set: Classic medallion set. There is nothing casual or spontaneous about this quilt. All is carefully planned to be formal, correct, with an element of the classical. Although each part is different from the rest, the whole has a feeling of order and cohesion.

Border: Multiple borders. Some patterns are deceptively simple, where these are deceptively complex. The entire quilt is much more of a feat than its effortless exterior suggests. The grapes are stuffed. The swag is one of the most beautiful we have seen. All the corner resolutions deserve study.

**WASHINGTON PLUME. 88″ x 96″, 1965-1980. Made by Elizabeth Harriman & Mary Schafer.
Cotton; polyester batting.**

This quilt could be called a "five-block" quilt, with its fifth block being cut in half. This kind of set was fairly common while quilts were made to be put on beds, but is almost never used today. Like "Tobacco Leaf," it refuses to fit the stereotype of an applique quilt. It is not light or flowery or delicate. It is aggresive and bold.

Set: We call this a four-block variation. What mattered to this quilt designer was how the quilt would work on the bed.

Border: This very dense applique vine fits on the fairly narrow border because the vine hardly moves. This is one of many three-sided border treatments, such as cutout corners, that are almost extinct.

WEEPING WILLOW. 34″ x 41½″, 1986. Made by the authors. Cotton; polyester batting.

This original design was drawn directly onto the chintz, cut out and appliqued onto the muslin ground, with no templates.

Set: This is the "pictorial" set, also thought of as a simple medallion.

Border: The sawtooth variation has no official name, but we call it the "flip-flop" sawtooth, for its bouncy movement. The outer, chintz border is quilted with a simple cable that stretches across the top and bottom, with the sides simply dropped in — no corner resolution.

WASHINGTON PLUME. 78″ x 90″, 1980. Made by the authors. Cotton; polyester batting.

We saw an old quilt like this in an antique store. Knowing we could never afford to buy it, we decided to make it instead. Gwen designed the block to be like those we have seen from around 1800-1850.

Set: This is the four-block set. Each block is thirty-two inches across. Alternate plumes have been quilted between the applique plumes.

Border: The swag did not look quite complete without the "knots," which we added last. This quilt, like most of those in this book, was made to go on a bed, which explains why the borders are wider on the top and bottom.

YOUNG MAN'S FANCY. *78" x 82", 1979.* **Made by the authors. Cotton; polyester batting.**

Here is an example of the set and border staying out of the way of a strong block design. The lattice is just wide enough to keep the blocks from interfering with one another, and the border is just wide enough to provide a simple frame for them.

Set: The blocks are set on the straight with lattice strips between. Nine-patch corner squares echo the large pieced blocks, adding the only other design element.

Border: The top and bottom whole-cloth borders are slightly wider at the top and bottom to fit the bed better.

Patterns

Sawtooth: short side of the triangle
Figures 1-17 made with this template.

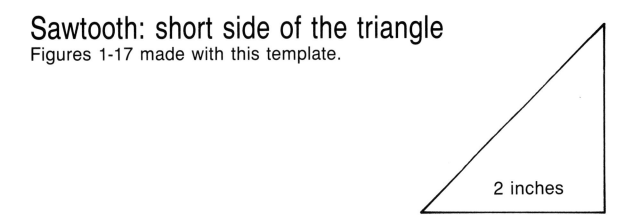

2 inches

Change directions in the middle to make corners work.

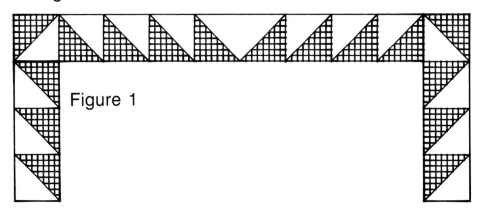

Figure 1

Otherwise, opposite corners will match.

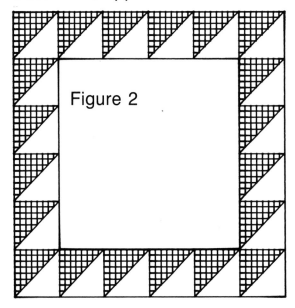

Figure 2

Another corner.
Figure 3

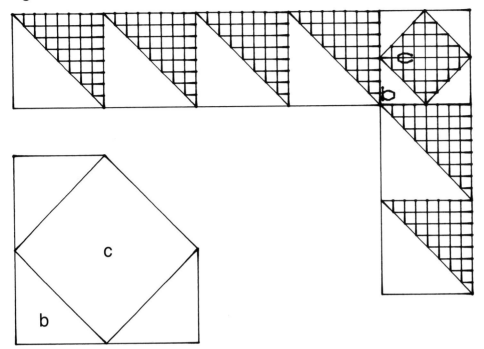

The "flip-flop" variation
Figure 4

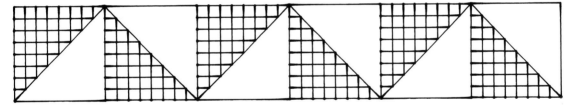

Random sawtooth
Figure 5

Double sawtooth borders
Triangles point in the same direction.
Figure 6

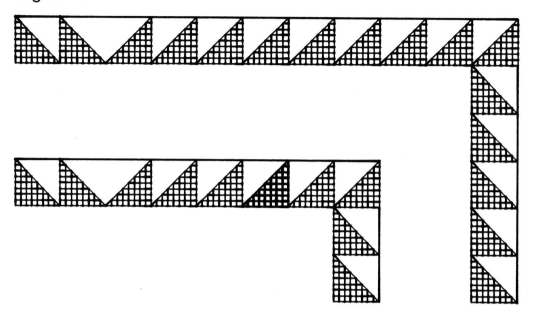

Triangles point in opposite directions.
Figure 7

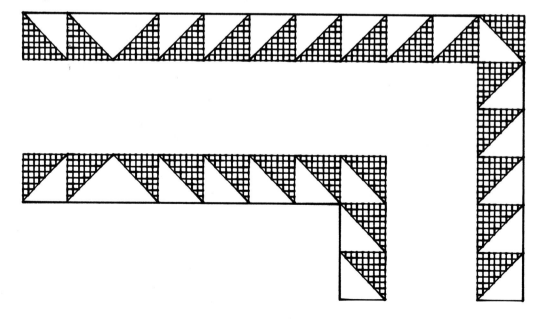

Color the middle for Tree Everlasting.
Figure 8

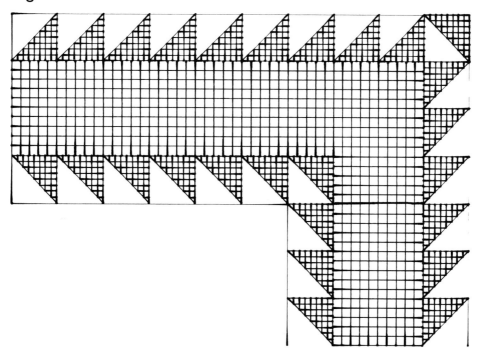

The triangles can be turned any way you want them.
Figure 9

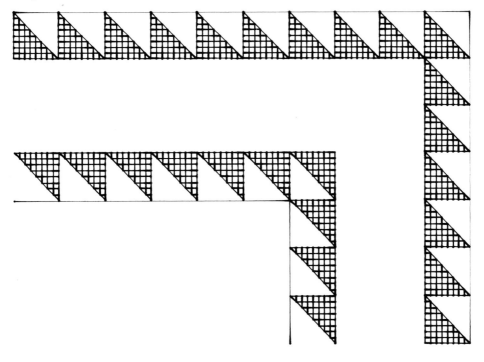

Triple Sawtooth border
Figure 10

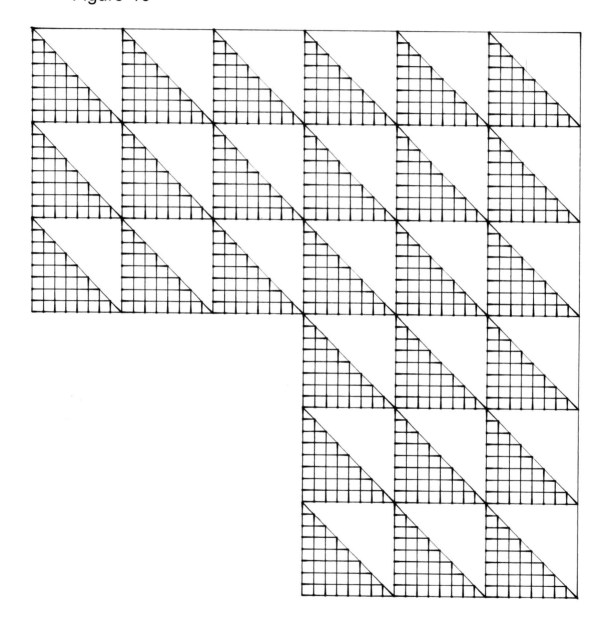

With this unit you can make many designs.
Here are six.

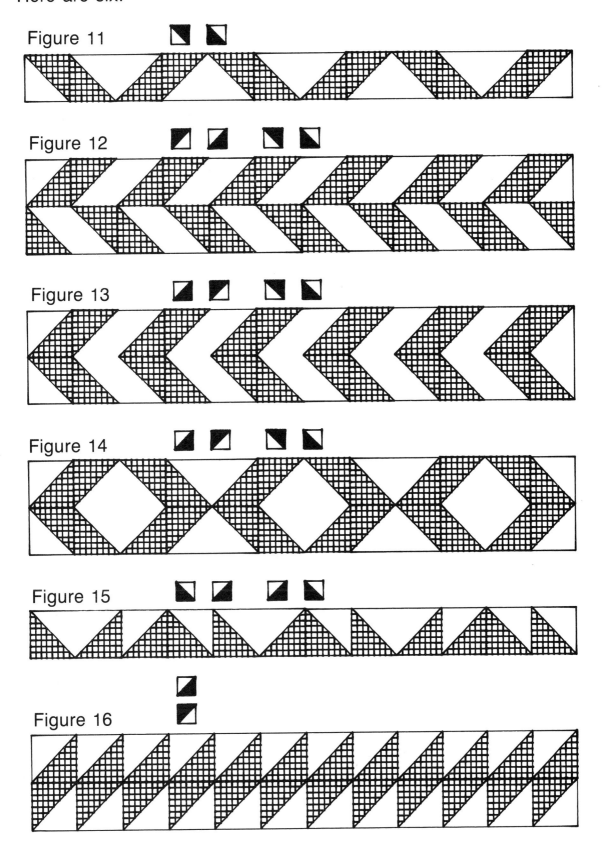

Figure 11

Figure 12

Figure 13

Figure 14

Figure 15

Figure 16

Sawtooth made of large and small triangles.
Figure 17

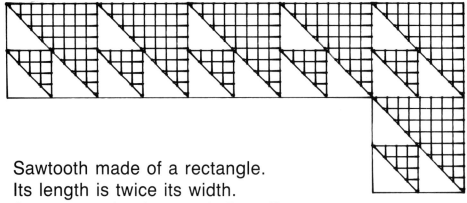

Sawtooth made of a rectangle.
Its length is twice its width.
Any rectangle gives a similar effect.
Figure 18

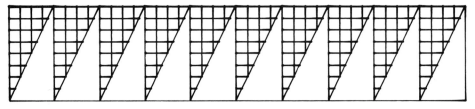

You can also divide the rectangle like this:
Figure 19

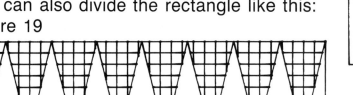

A rectangle 5 x 6 works like this at the corner.
Figure 20

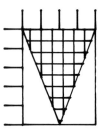

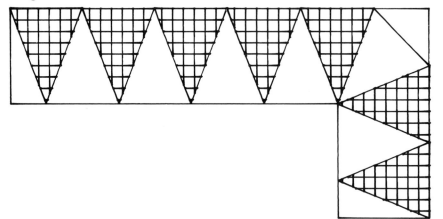

Figures 21-32 are made with the sawtooth on its long side.
Figures 21-27 are corners from old quilts.

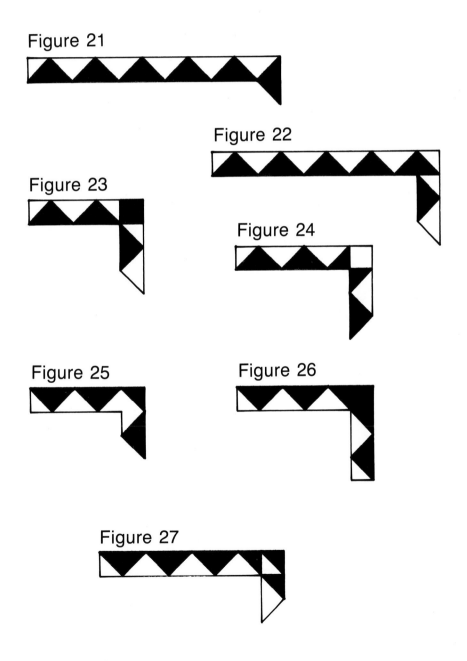

Figure 21

Figure 22

Figure 23

Figure 24

Figure 25

Figure 26

Figure 27

Double Sawtooth patterns

All triangles point inward.
Figure 20

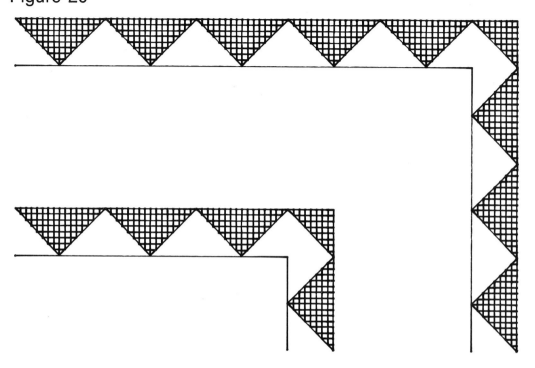

All triangles point toward each other.
Figure 29

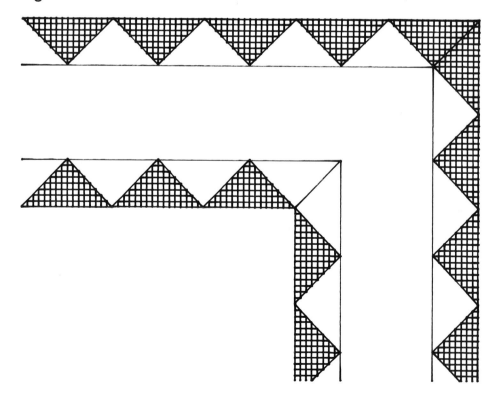

Same as Figure 29 with printed inner band.
Figure 30

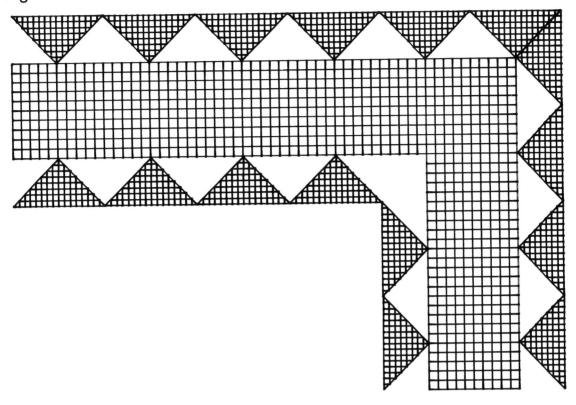

Triangles point away from each other.
Figure 31

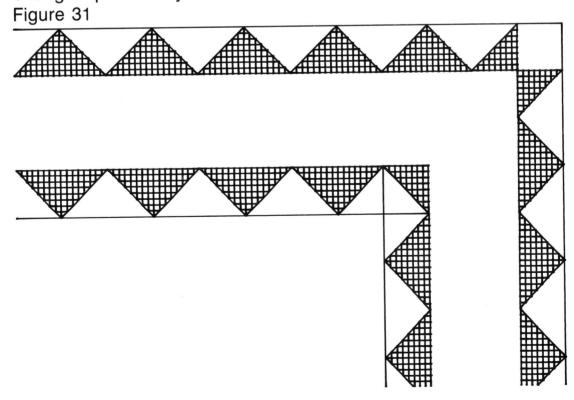

Sawtooth made with large and small triangles.
Figure 32

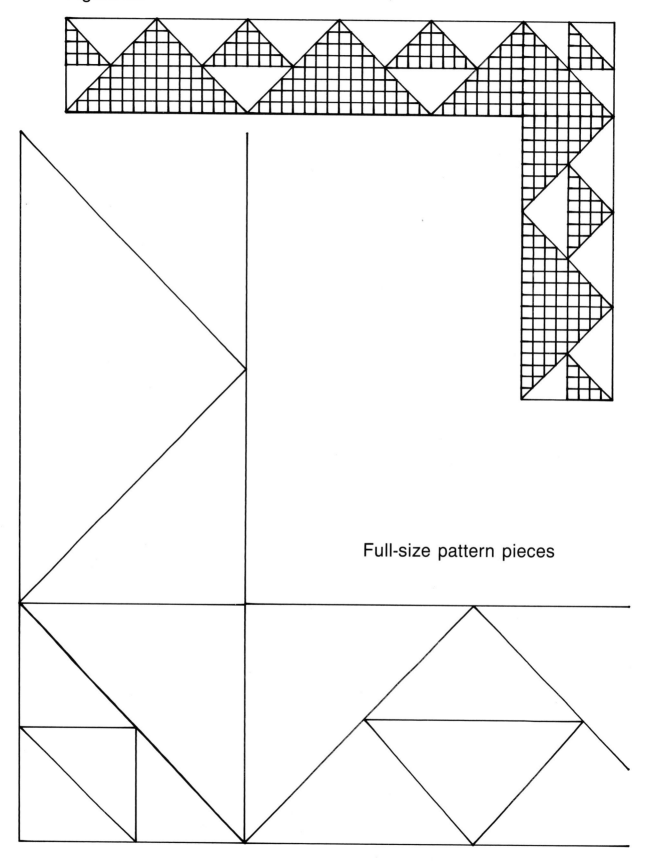

Full-size pattern pieces

Wild Goose Chase Borders
Triangles in one direction, no corner resolution.
Figure 33

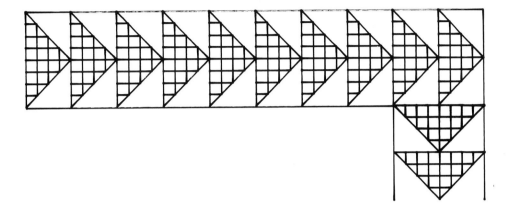

Triangles in one direction; resolve corners.
Figure 34.

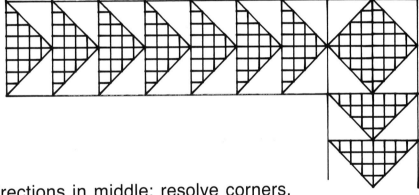

Change directions in middle; resolve corners.
Figure 35

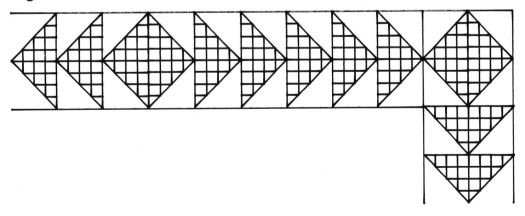

Double Wild Goose Chase with corner resolution.
Figure 36

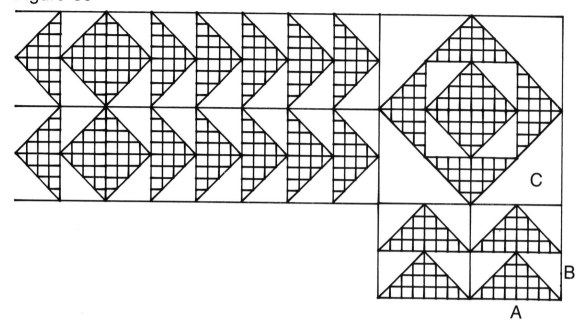

Pattern pieces for Wild Goose Chase borders.

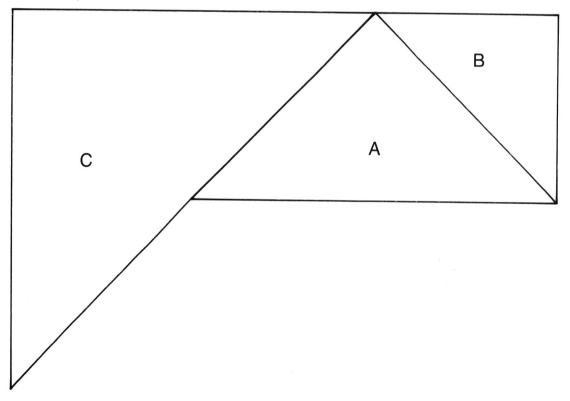

Gwen's Wild Goose Chase variation with pattern pieces.

Figure 37

Change directions in middle of border.

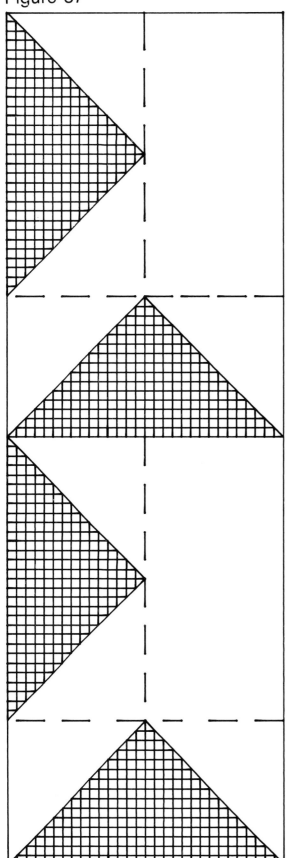

3-inch corner square.

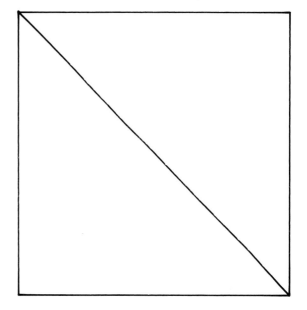

(One of our favorite borders!)

Wild Goose Chase and Sawtooth combination.
Figure 38

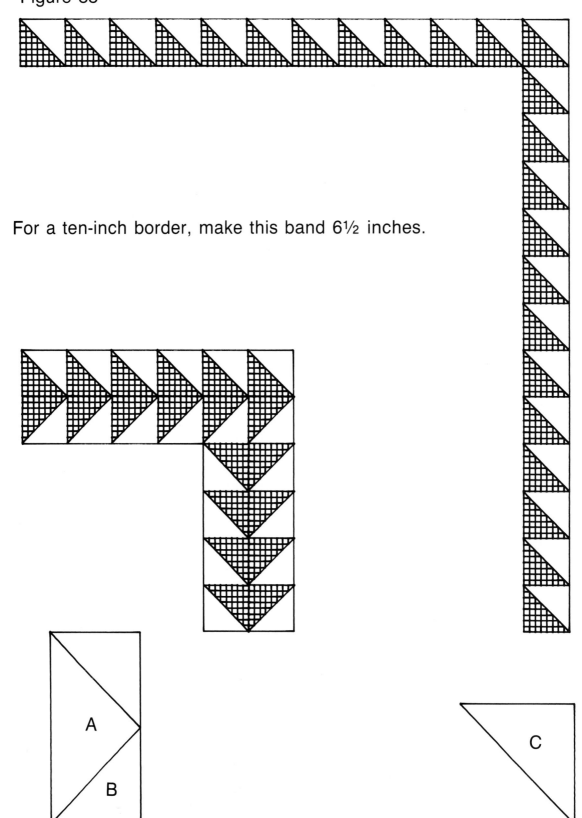

For a ten-inch border, make this band 6½ inches.

Two Delectable Mountain borders
Figure 39

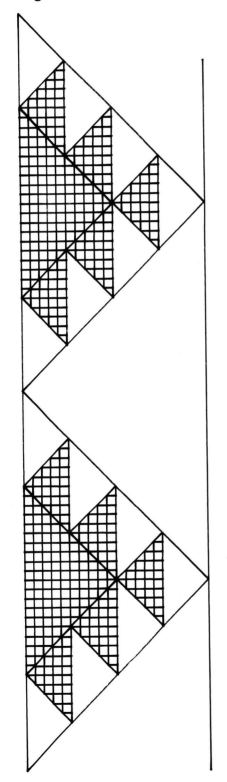

Figure 40

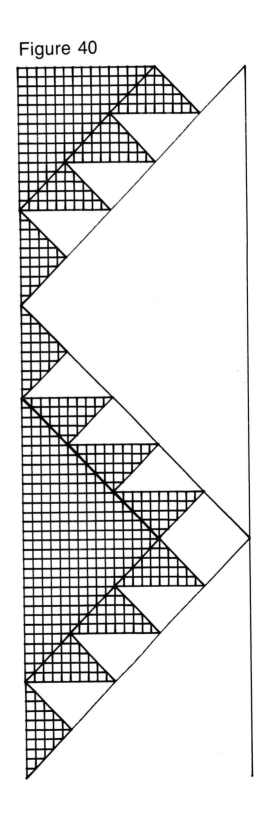

Diamond Borders, Single and Double
Figure 41

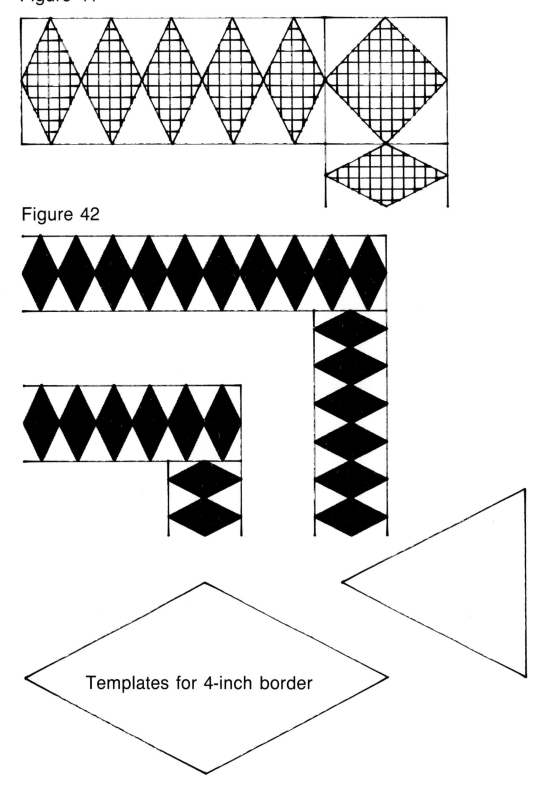

Figure 42

Templates for 4-inch border

Four-Patch Diamond borders.
Figure 43

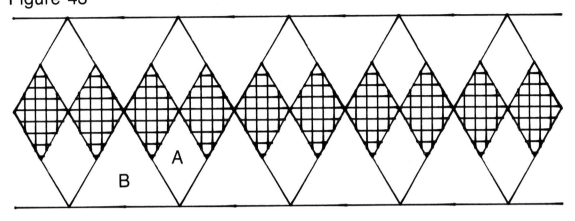

Figure 44

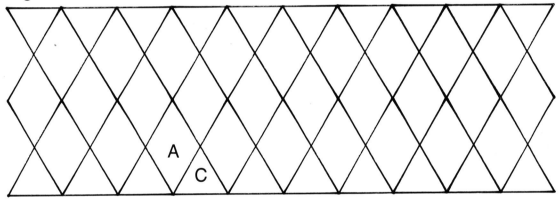

Templates for four-inch borders.

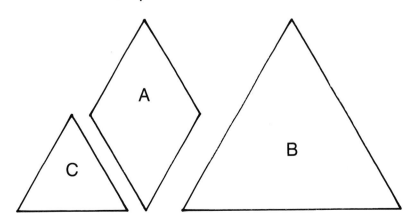

Lazy Diamonds
Figure 45

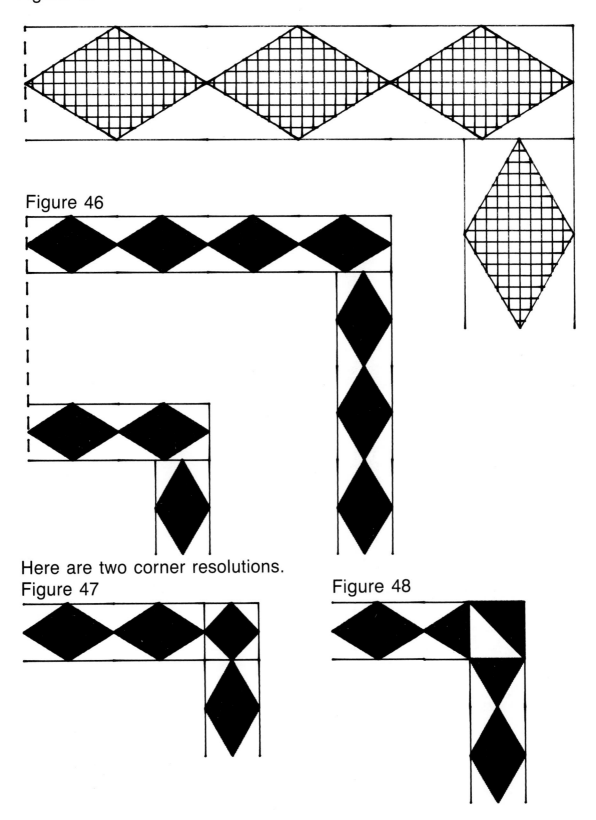

Figure 46

Here are two corner resolutions.
Figure 47

Figure 48

Squares

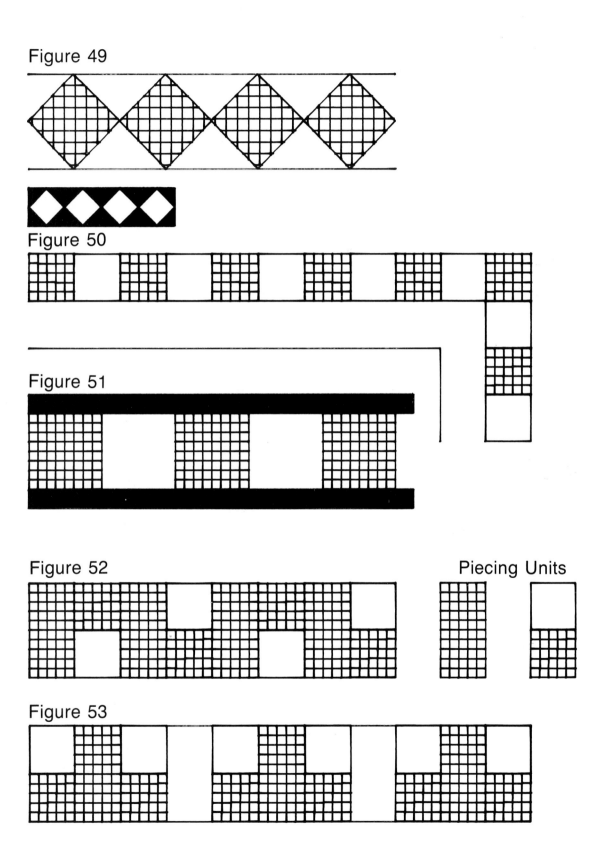

Figure 49

Figure 50

Figure 51

Figure 52

Piecing Units

Figure 53

Figure 54

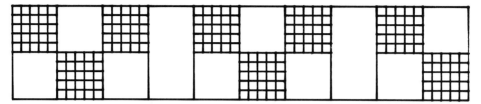

Figure 55

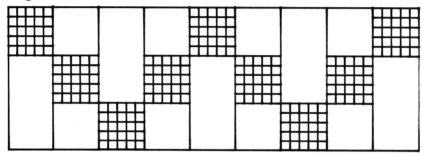

Figure 56

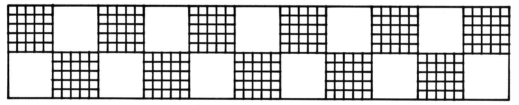

Figure 57

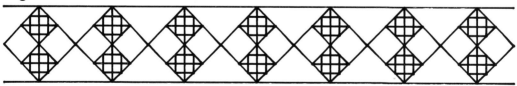

Figure 58

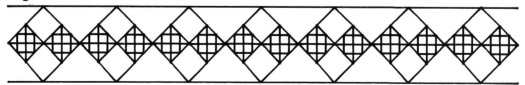

Streak of Lightning Borders
Figure 59

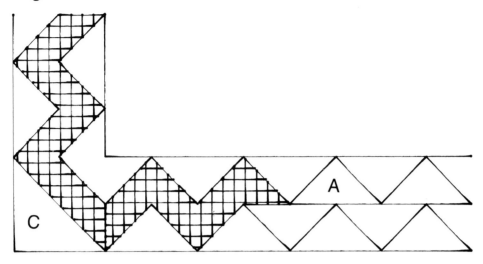

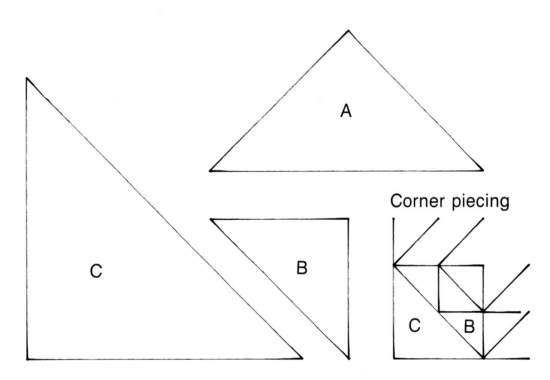

Corner piecing

Figure 60

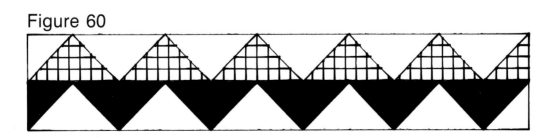

Streak of Lightning for Black Elegance.
Figure 61

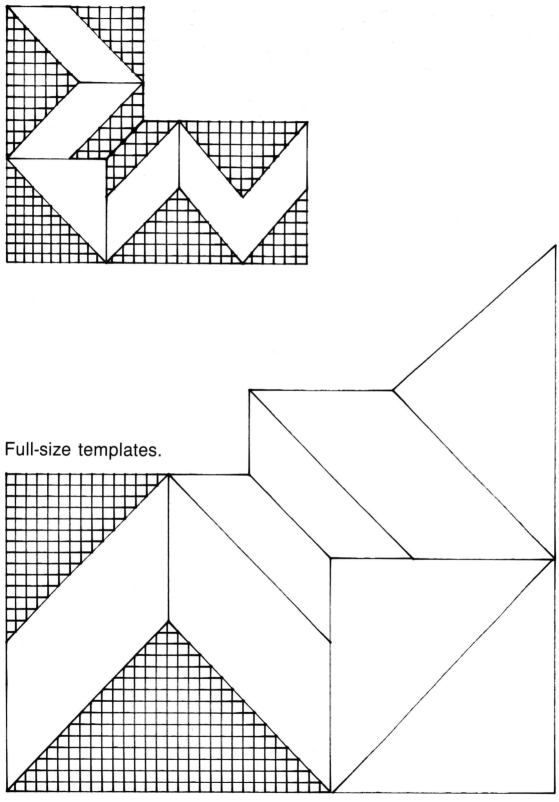

Full-size templates.

Figure 62

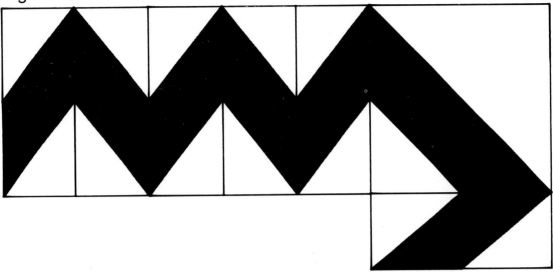

Streak of Lightning from Grandmother's Pride.
Figure 63

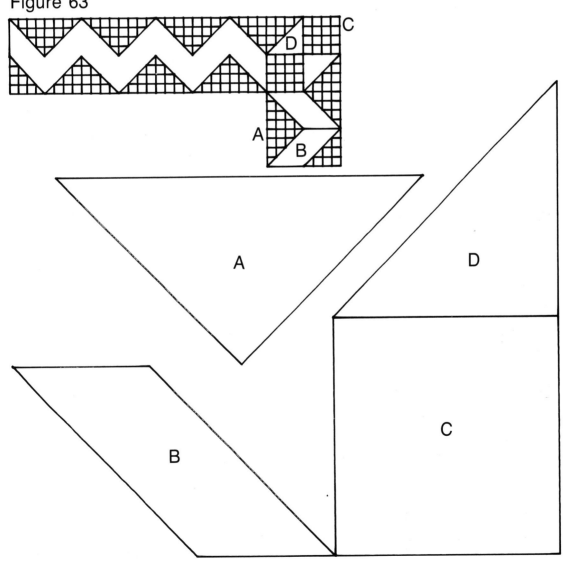

Strip Borders

Here are six simple strip-pieced borders from old quilts.

Figure 64

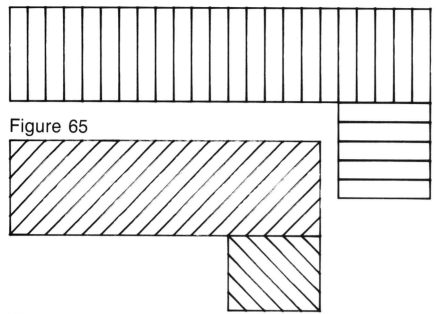

Figure 65

Figure 66

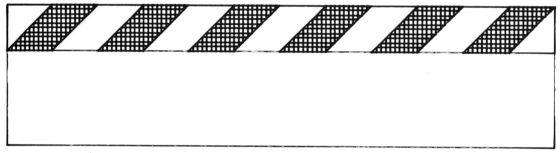

Figure 67

Figure 68

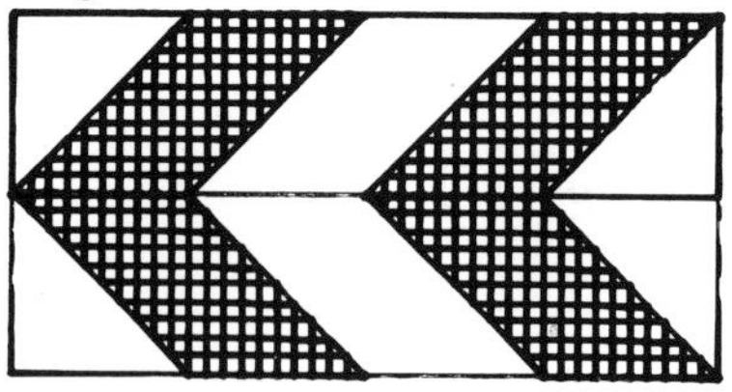

Figure 69

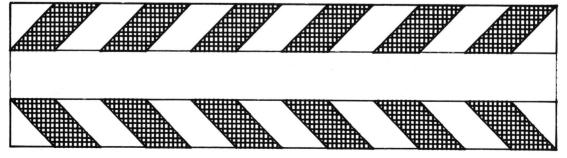

This is pieced from strip-pieced units.
Figure 70

Here are four borders made from block designs.
Figure 71 Pinwheel

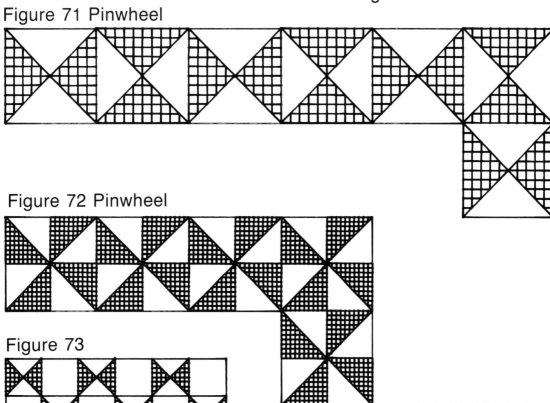

Figure 72 Pinwheel

Figure 73

Figure 74 Variable Star

Baby Blocks Border
Figure 75

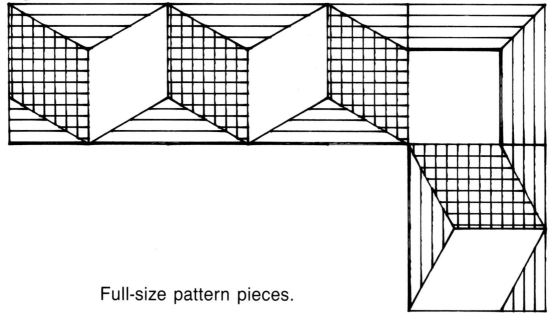

Full-size pattern pieces.

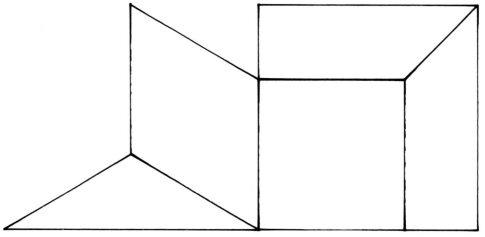

Braid
Figure 76

Full-size pattern pieces.

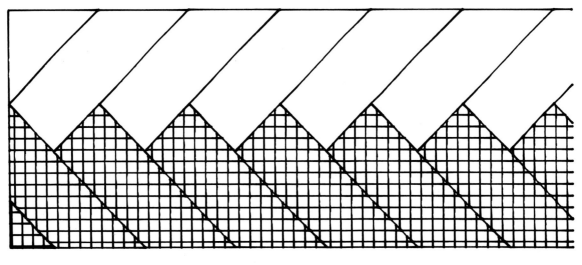

Squares and Triangles
Figure 77

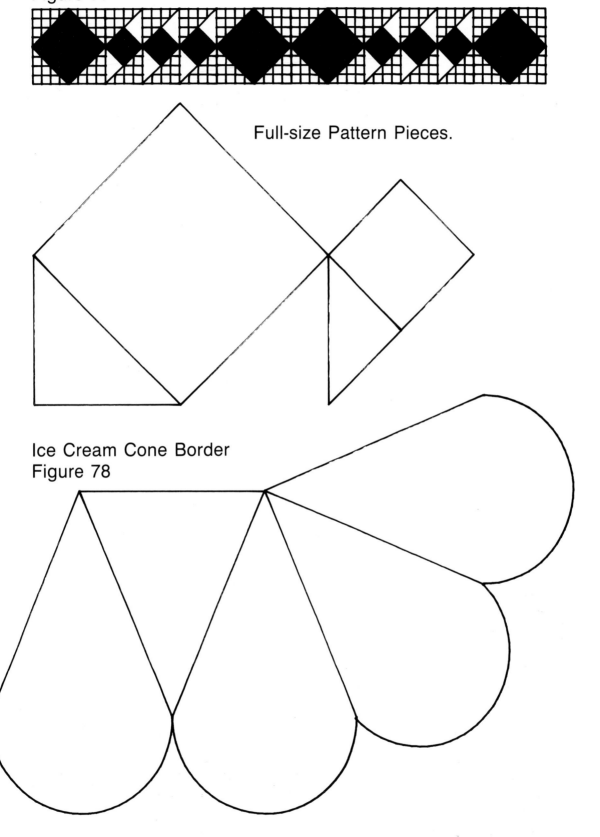

Full-size Pattern Pieces.

Ice Cream Cone Border
Figure 78

Linden Mill border pattern
Figure 79

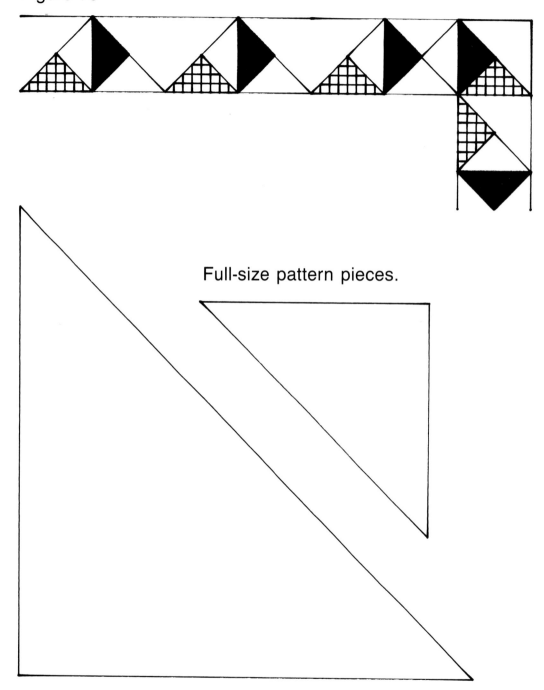

Full-size pattern pieces.

Single Chain and Knot border pattern.
Figure 60

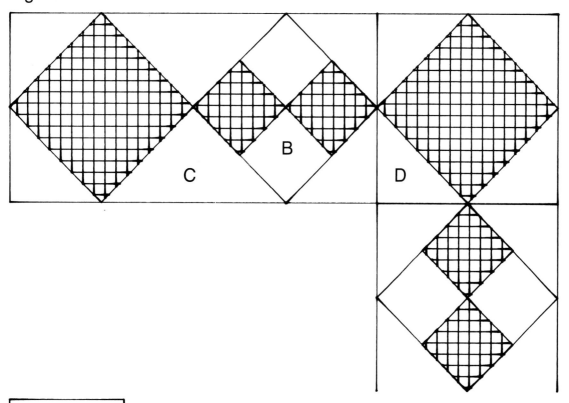

Full-size pattern pieces.

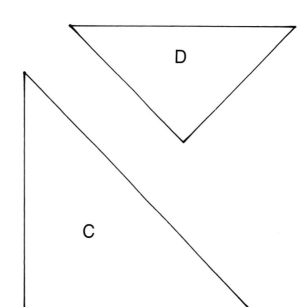

Lattice Patterns
Two ways to make plain lattice.
Figure 81

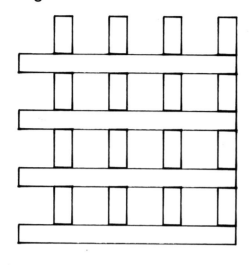

Figure 82

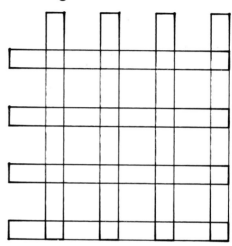

With corner squares.
Figure 83

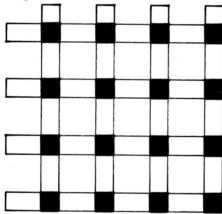

With end squares.
Figure 84

Corner blocks taken from old quilts

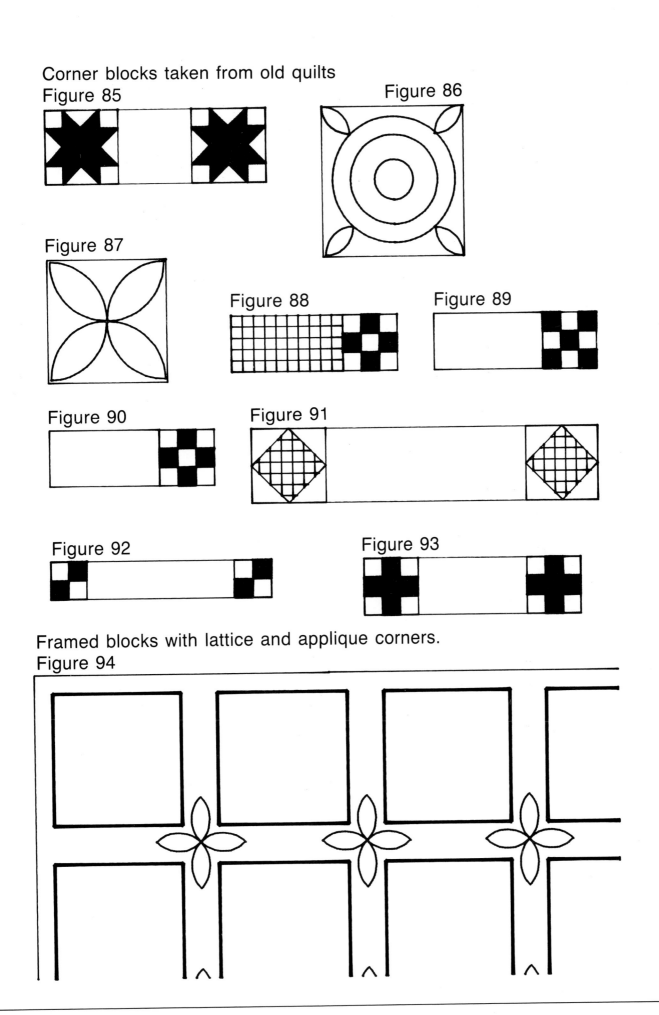

Figure 85

Figure 86

Figure 87

Figure 88

Figure 89

Figure 90

Figure 91

Figure 92

Figure 93

Framed blocks with lattice and applique corners.
Figure 94

Here are six three-strip lattice designs with corners taken from old quilts.

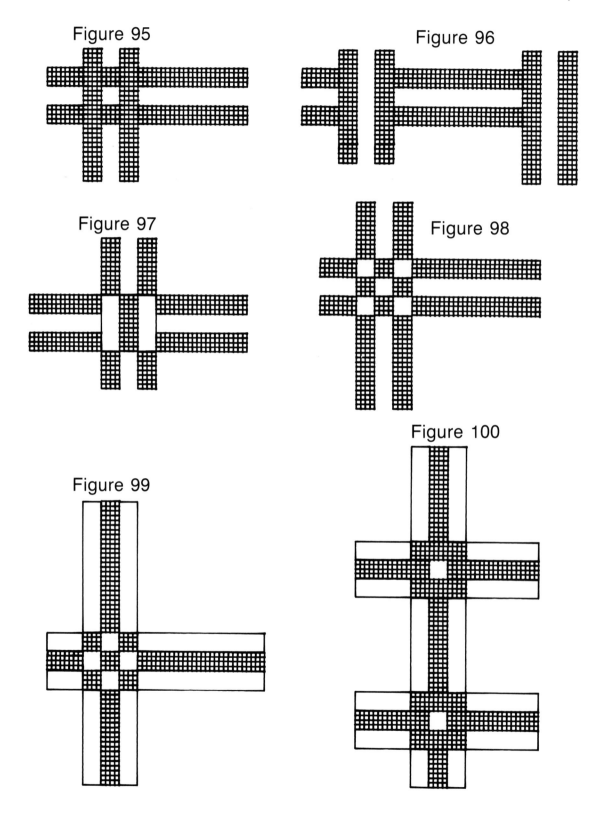

Figure 95

Figure 96

Figure 97

Figure 98

Figure 99

Figure 100

Sawtooth Lattice Patterns.

Figure 101

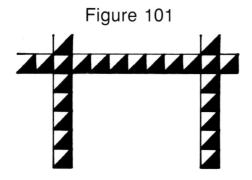

Figure 102

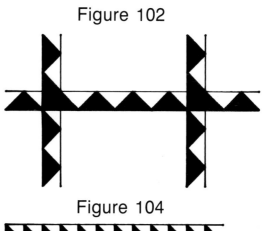

Figure 103

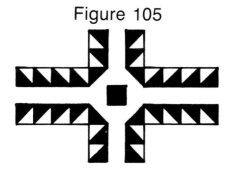

Figure 104

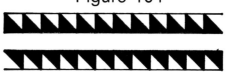

Figure 105

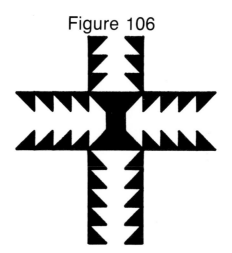

Figure 106

Figure 107

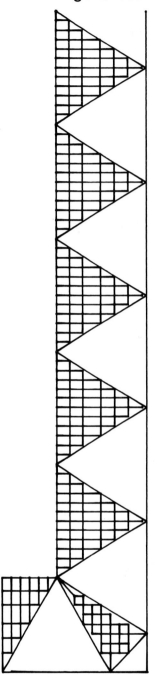

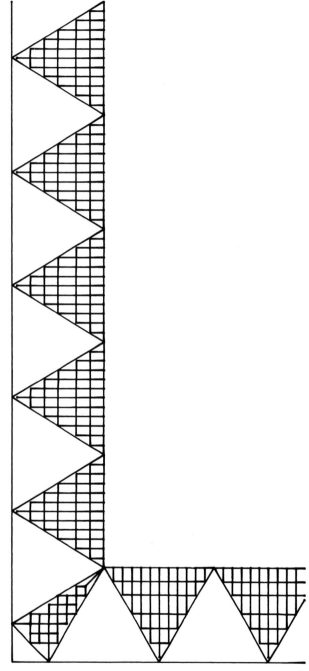

Optional corner resolution.

Figure 108

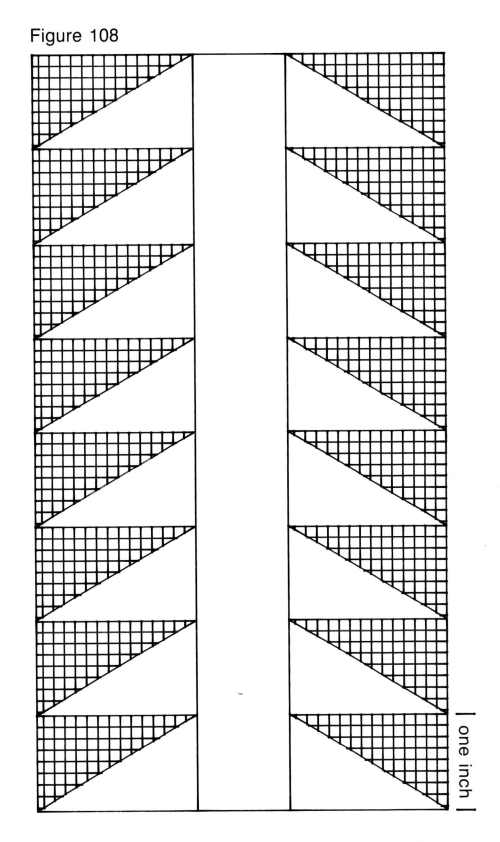

one inch

This sawtooth lattice pattern is one inch wide for easy resolution on even-size blocks.

Figure 109

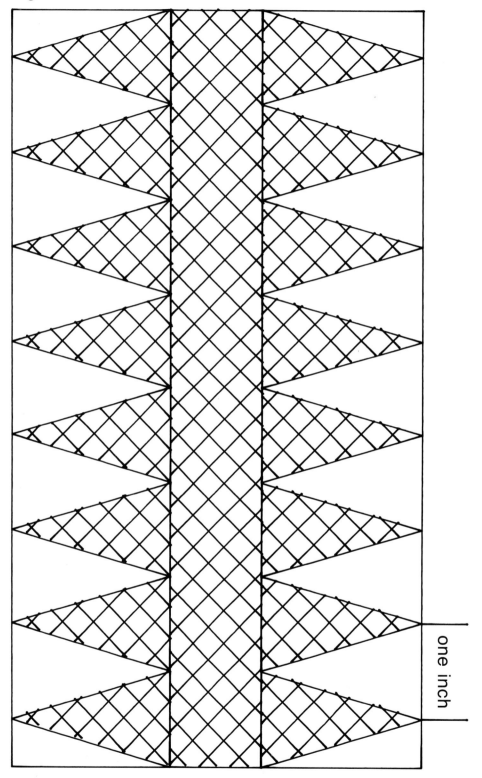

one inch

Wild Goose Chase Lattice

These can all be made with
this inch-wide template.

Figure 110

Figure 111

Figure 112

Figure 113

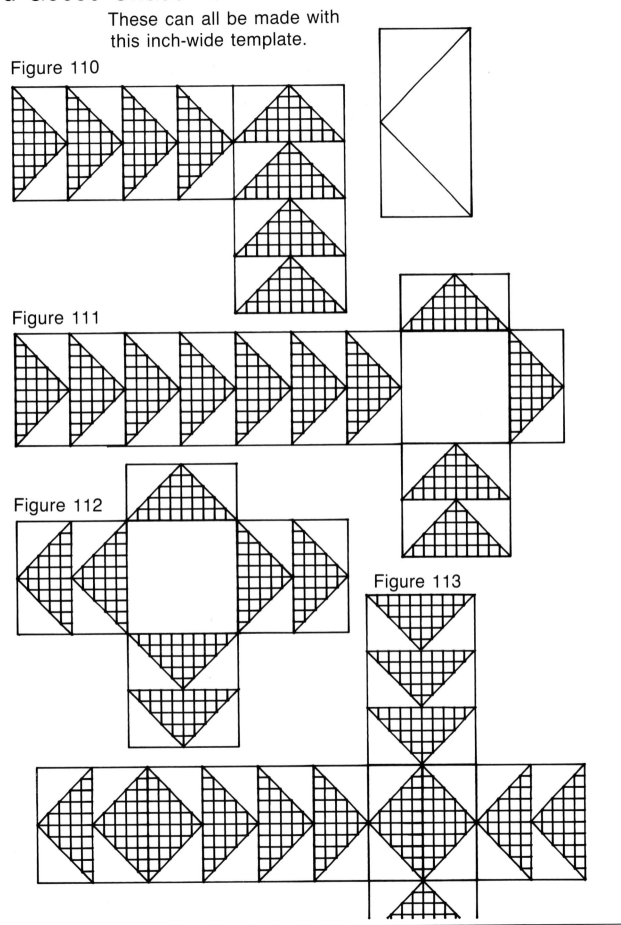

Diamond Lattice Patterns

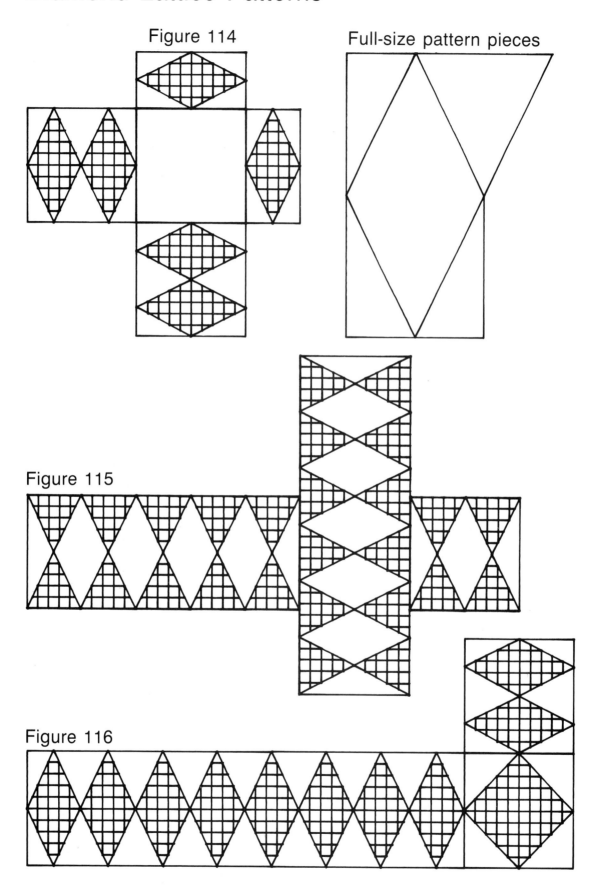

Figure 114

Full-size pattern pieces

Figure 115

Figure 116

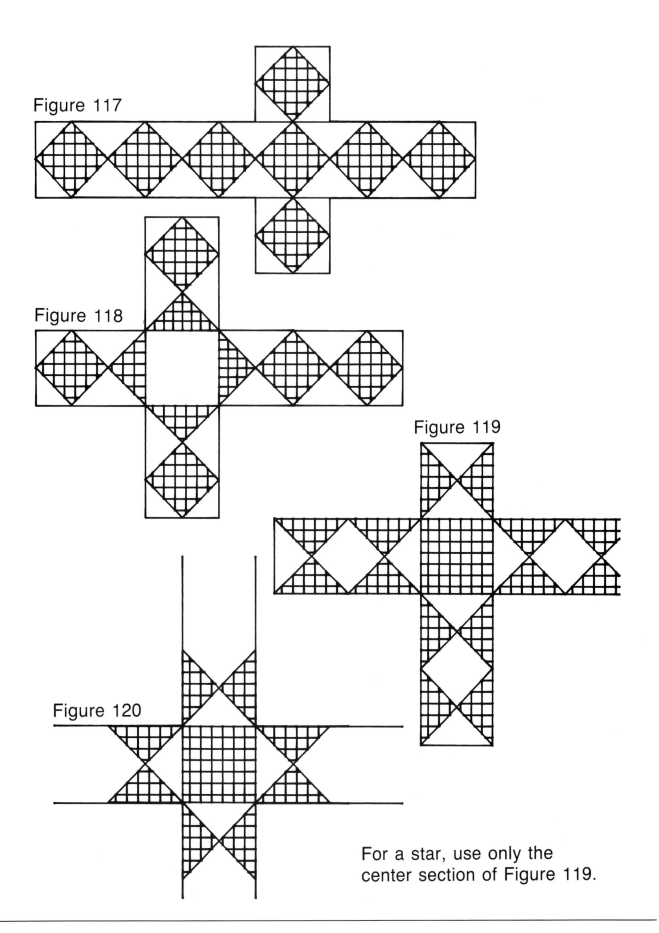

Figure 117

Figure 118

Figure 119

Figure 120

For a star, use only the center section of Figure 119.

This lattice strip can be any length or width.
By changing the light and dark, many designs are possible.

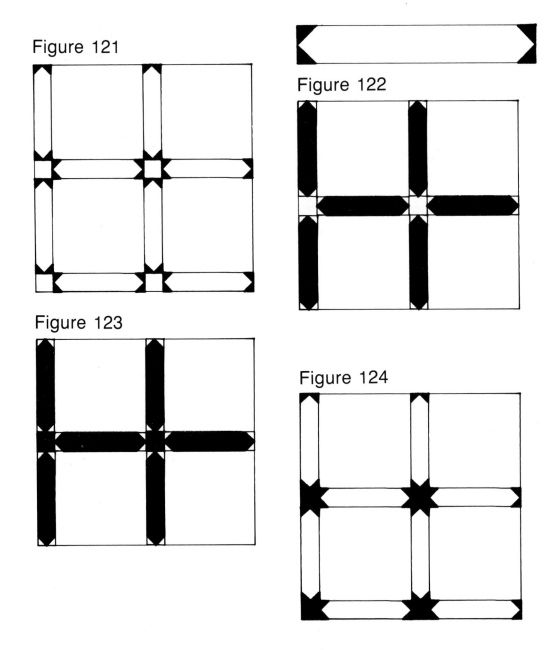

Figure 121

Figure 122

Figure 123

Figure 124

Garden Maze
Figure 125

Bibliography

Bishop, Robert. *New Discoveries in American Quilts*. New York: E.P. Dutton and Company, Inc., 1975.

Bishop, Robert, William Secord, and Judith Reiter Weissman. *Quilts, Coverlets, Rugs & Samplers*. New York: Alfred A. Knopf, 1982.

Brackman, Barbara. *An Encyclopedia of Pieced Quilt Patterns*. Lawrence, Kansas: Prairie Flower Publishing, 1979.

Carlisle, Lillian Baker. *Pieced Work and Applique Quilts at the Shelbourne Museum*. Shelbourne Museum pamphlet series #2. Shelbourne, VT., 1957.

Colby, Averil. *Patchwork Quilts*. New York: Charles Scribner's Sons, 1965.

_____. *Quilting*. New York: Charles Scribner's Sons, 1971.

Cooper, Patricia and Norma Bradley Buferd. *The Quilters*. New York: Anchor Press/Doubleday, 1978.

Curtis, Phillip H. *American Quilts in the Newark Museum Collection*. Newark, NJ. The Newark Museum, 1974.

Finley, Ruth E. *Old Patchwork Quilts and the Women Who Made Them*. Newton Centre, Massachusetts: Charles T. Branford Company, 1970.

Fitzrandolph, Mavis. *Traditional Quilting*. London: B.T. Batsford, Ltd., 1954.

Fox, Sandi. *19th Century American Patchwork Quilt*. The Seibu Museum of Art. Japan. 1983-1984.

Haders, Phyllis. *The Warner Collector's Guide to American Quilts*. New York: Warner Books, Inc. 1981.

Hall, Carrie A., and Rose Kretsinger. *The Romance of the Patchwork Quilt in America*. Coldwell, Idaho: Caxton Printers Ltd., Bonanza Books, 1935.

Havig, Bettina. *Missouri Heritage Quilts*. Paducah, Kentucky: American Quilter's Society, 1986.

Holstein, Jonathan. *The Pieced Quilt an American Design Tradition*. Boston, Mass.: New York Graphic Society, 1973.

Houck, Carter and Myron Miller. *American Quilts and How To Make Them*. New York: Charles Scribner's Sons, 1975.

Ickis, Marguerite. *The Standard Book of Quilt-Making and Collection*. New York: Dover Publishers, Inc., 1949.

James, Michael. *The Quiltmaker's Handbook*. Englewood Cliffs, New Jersey: Prentice-Hall, Inc., 1978.

Kentucky Quilts Project, The. *Kentucky Quilts 1800-1900*. New York: Pantheon Books, 1982.

Kiracofe, Roderick and Michael Kile. *The Quilt Digest*. San Francisco: Kiracofe and Kile, 1983 and 1985.

Lane, Rose Wilder. *Woman's Day Book of American Needlework*. New York: Simon and Schuster, 1963.

Lasansky, Jeannette. *In the Heart of Pennsylvania 19th and 20th Century Quiltmaking Traditions*. Lewisburg, Pennsylvania: Oral Traditions Project. 1985.

McKim, Ruby. *101 Patchwork Patterns*. Dover Publishers, Inc., 1962.

Nelson, Cyril I. *The Quilt Engagement Calendar*. New York: E.P. Dutton, 1975, 1979-1986.

Orlofsky, Patsy & Myron. *Quilts in America*. New York: McGraw-Hill Book Company, 1974.

Peto, Florence. *American Quilts and Coverlets*. New York: Chanticleer Press, 1949.

_____. *Historic Quilts*. New York: The American Historical Company, Inc. 1939.

Safford, Carleton L., and Robert Bishop. *America's Quilts and Coverlets*. New York: E.P. Dutton and Company, Inc., 1972.

Sexton, Carlie. *Old Fashioned Quilts*. 1928. Reprinted by Barbara Bannister, 1964.

_____. *Yesterday's Quilts in Homes of Today*. 1930. Reprinted by Barbara Bannister, 1964.

Walker, Michele. *The Complete Book of Quiltmaking*. New York: Alfred A. Knopf, 1986.

Webster, Marie D. *Quilts—Their Story and How to Make Them*. Tudor Publishing Company, 1948. Doubleday, Page and Company, 1915.

References

This reference is provided as an additional resource. Examples of many of the patterns in this book can be found in books listed in the bibliography. We cannot list a source for every pattern as some do not appear in readily available sources or they were collected from individual and unpublished quilts. The sources are indicated by the authors name only, except when the author has two books listed in the bibliography in which case the book title is given in abbreviation. In the case of musum catalogs we cite the name of the museum. The Quilt Engagement Calenders are listed as Q.E.C. followed by the year. When the same quilt is shown in two books we list both sources.

Fig. 1   Bishop. (New Discoveries in A.Q.) #58.
Fig. 2   Nelson and Houck, plate #161
          Q.E.C. 1975, #27
Fig. 3   Q.E.C. 1982, #19
Fig. 4   Holstein, Fig. 9
          *Additional sources for borders with
          sawtooth resting on short side:*
          Holstein, plates 7, 15, 30, 46, 62
          Bishop, (New Discoveries in A.Q.) #39,
             40, 95
          Nelson and Houck, #161, 174
          Newark Museum, p. 8
          Lasansky, pp. 1, 5, 37, 44, 46, 48, 49, 53,
             57, 64, 77, 93
          Sexton, (Old F.Q.) p. 21
          Finley, plates 9, 22, 59, 63
          Webster, pp. 20, 33, 84
          Orlofsky, plate 18. Figures 72, 153
Fig. 9   Holstein, plate 2
          *Additional sources for borders with **double**
          sawtooth resting on short side:*
          Q.E.C. 1985, #13
          Safford and Bishop, #153
          Orlofsky, Figures 36, 46
Fig. 10   Holstein, fig. 12
          Safford and Bishop, #219
          Bishop (New Discoveries in A.Q.) #38
Fig. 12   Nelson and Houck, #72
Fig. 16   Q.E.C. 1982, #26
Fig. 18   Bishop, (New Discoveries in A.Q.) #55
Fig. 19   Safford and Bishop #220
          Q.E.C. 1985, #39
Fig. 20   Houck and Miller, plates 138, 165
          Q.E.C. 1986, #31
          The Newark Museum, pp. 6, 26
          Finley, plates 60, 62
          Orlofsky, plates 23, 77
Fig. 21   Q.E.C. 1985, #12
Fig. 23   Holstein, plate 82
Fig. 24   Holstein, plate82
Fig. 25   Q.E.C. 1979 #1
Fig. 26   Bishop, (New Discvoveries in A.Q.), #96
          Additional sources showing variations:
          Q.E.C. 1985, #54
          Q.E.C. 1975, #15
          Orlofsky, plate7
          The Quilters, p. 141
          Safford and Bishop, #109, 114, 124, 159,
             199
          Orlofsky, plates 58, 74
Fig. 29   Q.E.C. 1980, #54
          Q.E.C. 1981, #10, #25
Fig. 32   Houck and Miller, plate 86
Fig. 33   Q.E.C. 1986, #56
Fig. 34   Q.E.C. 1982, #18
          Newark Museum, pg. 42
Fig. 35   Holstein, Fig. 14
          Bishop, (New Discoveries in A.Q.), #12
          Orlofsky, fig. 176
          Lasansky, p. 71 (variation)
Fig. 36   Q.E.C. 1984, #19
Fig. 38   Nelson and Houck, #10
Fig. 39   Q.E.C. 1983, #46
Fig. 40   Orlofsky, plate 8
          Bishop, (New Discoveries in A.Q.), #116
Fig. 41   Fox, plate 4
          Q.E.C. 1985, #11
          Q.E.C. 1975, #13
          Bishop, (New Discoveries in A.Q.), #151

Fig. 42   Sexton (Yesterdays Q)
          Q.E.C. 1979, #56
Fig. 44   Quilt Digest, 1983. p. 41
          Q.E.C. 1985, #147
Fig. 49   Webster, p. 38
          Q.E.C. 1975, #2
          Q.E.C. 1981, #50
          Nelson and houck, #141
          Q.E.C. 1986, #19 (color variation)
          Lasansky, pp. 34, 72 (color variation)
Fig. 50   Webster, p. 56
          Q.E.C. 1985, #23
          Holstein, plate 89
Fig. 51   Bishop, (New Discoveries in A.Q.), #48
Fig. 52   Nelson and Houck, #173
          Sexton, (Old Fashioned Q) p.6
Fig. 53   Nelson and Houck, #77
          The Newark Museum, p46
Fig. 59   Nelson and Houck, #76
          Holstein, plate 75
          Q.E.C. 1975, #30, 45
          Q.E.C. 1981, #33
          Q.E.C. 1985, #49
          Bishop, (New Discoveries in A.Q.), #65
          Nelson and Houck, #77
          Additional sources with variations:
          Safford and Bishop, #135, 154
          Lasansky, p.9
          Webster, p. 112
          Orlofsky, fig. 152
Fig. 60   Lasansky, p. 36
Fig. 62   Q.E.C. 1985, #51
Fig. 64-65 Bishop, (New Discoveries in A.Q.), #29
          Fox, 27
          Holstein, plate 9
          Q.E.C. 1975, #56
          Q.E.C. 1979, #16
          Q.E.C. 1980, #12
          Q.E.C. 1983, #45
          Q.E.C. 1986, #15
Fig. 66   Lasansky, p. 53
          Holstein, plate 87
Fig. 67   Q.E.C. 1981, #47
Fig. 68   Q.E.C. 1975, #22
          Safford and Bishop, #132
Fig. 69   Nelson and Houck, #158
Fig. 70   Q.E.C. 1981, #48
Fig. 71   Holstein, plate66
Fig. 72   Holstein, fig. 15
Fig. 73   Bishop, #164 (New Discoveries in A.Q.)
Fig. 74   Nelson and Houck, #144
Fig. 75   Nelson and Houck, #140
          Q.E.C. 1980, #3
Fig. 77   Nelson and Houck, #164
          Q.E.C. 1975, #14
Fig. 78   Safford and Bishop, #157
          Sexton, (Old Fashioned Q) p.2
          Lattice patterns . . . . . .
Fig. 81-82 Sexton, (Old Fashioned Q) p.8
(Plain   Webster, p.85
lattice)   Finley, plates 41, 52, 60, 91
          Orlofsky, plates 19, 102, 103. Figures 82,
             146.
          Q.E.C. 1975, #12, 41
          Q.E.C. 1979, #4, 23, 48
          Q.E.C. 1980, #10, 43
          Q.E.C. 1981, #10
          Q.E.C. 1984, #55, 50
          Houck and Miller, pp. 53, 116, 195

          Holstein, plates 6, 17, 65, 80, 81. Fig. 40
          Lasansky, pp. 61, 73
          Bishop (New Discoveries in A.Q.), #56,
             60, 69, 127
          Quilt Digest, 1985. pg. 58
          Safford and Bishop, #144, 154, 185, 188,
             232, 264, 300, 301, 310
          Havig, p. 52
          Hall and Kretsinger, pp. 182, 231.
Fig. 83   Orlofsky, plate 90
          Finley, plate 11
          Houck and Miller, p. 178
          Holstein, figures 3, 17, 31. Plates 18, 79
          Lasansky, pg. 46
          Bishop (New Discoveries in A.Q.), #53,
             73, 125
          Havig, pp. 8, 26
          Quilt Digest, 1985. pp. 62, 64-68
          Safford and Bishop, #109, 141, 156, 167,
             223, 229, 290, 316, 325
          Q.E.C. 1975, #45, 46
          Q.E.C. 1979, #17
          Q.E.C. 1980, #41
          Q.E.C. 1983, #37
          Q.E.C. 1984, #1, 10
          Q.E.C. 1986, #49
Fig. 84   Q.E.C. 1982, #2
Fig. 85   Houck and Miller, p. 151
Fig. 87   Holstein, plate 5
Fig. 88   Lasansky, p. 71
          Kentucky Quilts Project, plate 4
Fig. 90   Nelson and Houck, #153
          Hall and Kretsinger, p. 222
Fig. 92   Quilt Digest, 1985. p. 32
Fig. 94   Holstein, plate 5
Fig. 95   Finley, plate 21
Fig. 96   The Newark Museum, p. 48
          Houck and Miller, p. 71
          Safford and Bishop, #147, 244
Fig. 97   Q.E.C. 1984, #45
Fig. 98   Safford and Bishop, #169, 157
Fig. 99   Sexton, (Old Fashioned Q). p. 11
          Lane, p. 96
Fig. 101 Q.E.C. 1980, #56
          Safford and Bishop, #295
          Hall and Kretsinger, p. 241
Fig. 103 Hall and Kretsinger, p. 194
Fig. 104 Fox, plate 1
          Nelson and Houck, #18
Fig. 105 Kentucky Quilts Project, plate 47
Fig. 107 Q.E.C. 1985, #12
Fig. 108 Q.E.C. 1985, #339
Fig. 109 Safford and Bishop, #134
          Q.E.C. 1975, #10
          Orlofsky, plate 20
Fig. 110 Quilt Digest, 1983, p. 36
          Safford and Bishop, #106 (variation)
Fig. 115 Bishop, (New Discoveries in A.Q.), #150
Fig. 117 Webster, p. 75
          Finley, plate 22
          Q.E.C., 1975, #2
          Houck and Miller, p. 178
Fig. 118 Q.E.C. 1981, #50
Fig. 123 Quilt Digest, p.33
Fig. 125 Garden Maze Variations:
          The Newark Museum, p. 50
          Missouri Quilt Project, p. 76
          Finley, plates 54, 71
          Lane, p. 95
          Orlofsky, figures 49, 205

Index of Quilt Names